Learn to Draw Manga Anatomy Fundamentals

Simplified Manga style anatomy

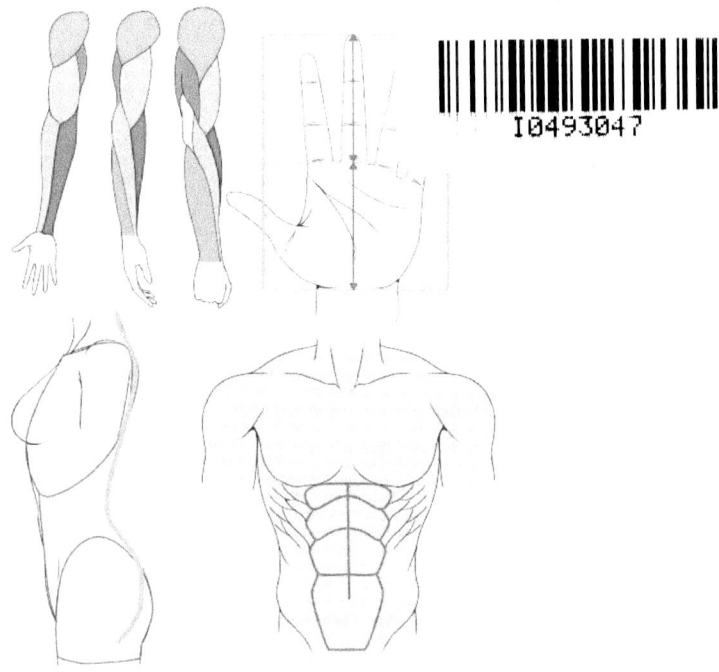

Learn to Draw Series

William T. Dela Peña Jr.

Mendon Cottage Books

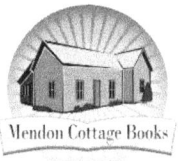

JD-Biz Publishing

Our books are available at

1. Amazon.com
2. Barnes and Noble
3. Itunes
4. Kobo
5. Smashwords
6. Google Play Books

Download Free Books!

http://MendonCottageBooks.com

Table of Contents

INTRODUCTION

Are you struggling with drawing the human figure or sometimes you find your drawing so stiff and not so organic? If yes, This book will help you to find the answers and help you to overcome it.

The human body has a complex structure that can be difficult to understand. Drawing it can be very confusing without a basic understanding of human anatomy.

This book will help you to understand the human anatomy in a simplified manner that can be easy and comfortable for beginners. In this book, you will learn the step by step drawing process and some techniques that will really help you to understand the human anatomy fundamentals.

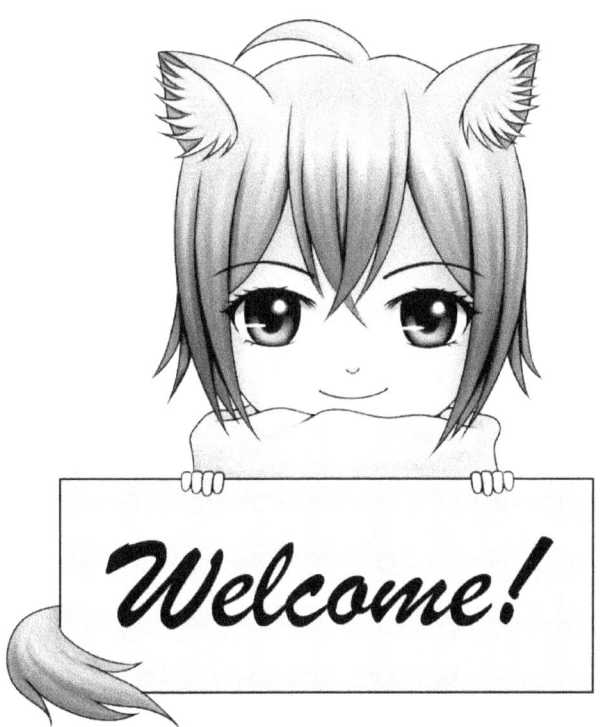

STRUCTURE OF A MANGA BODY AND PROPORTION

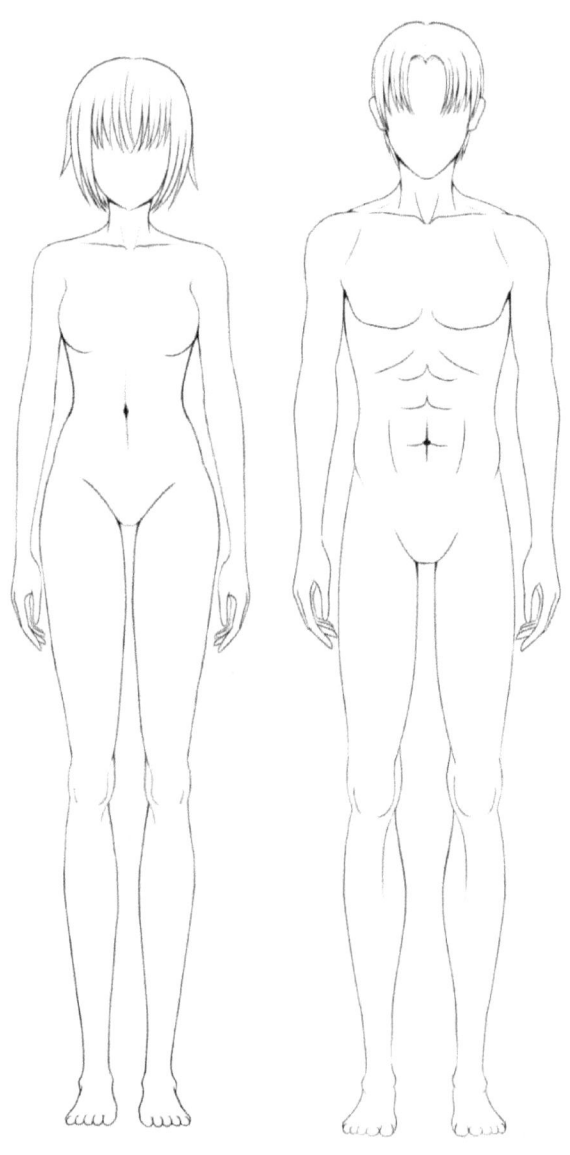

THE FEMALE MANGA PROPORTION

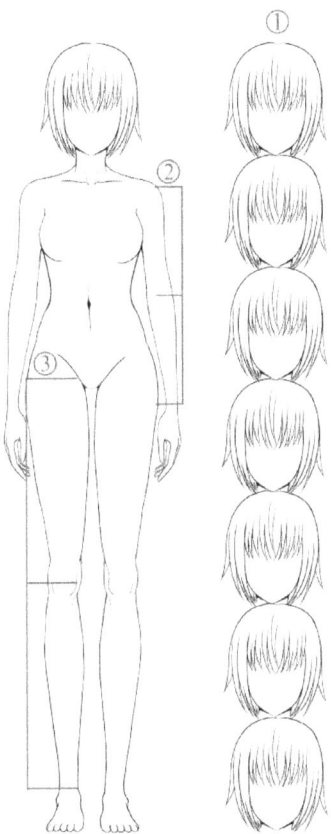

1. The female Manga Proportion varies from six to seven heads tall. In this tutorial I use seven heads tall, the crotch is located below the third head above, and always remember when drawing a female body always make the legs longer than the torso.

2. The upper and lower portion of the arms are equal in length and the elbow is located halfway.

3. The upper leg and lower leg are equal in length and the knee is located halfway.

THE MALE MANGA PROPORTION

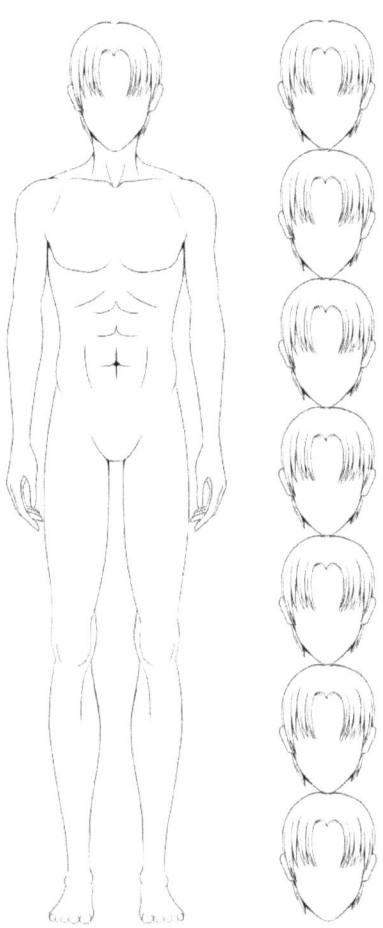

The standard male manga proportion based on the head unit is equal to seven heads tall the only difference of male proportion to the female, is the location of the crotch. The male crotch is lower than female and as a result, the length of the torso of the male is longer than the torso of a female.

HOW TO DRAW A FEMALE TORSO IN THREE DIFFERENT VIEWS

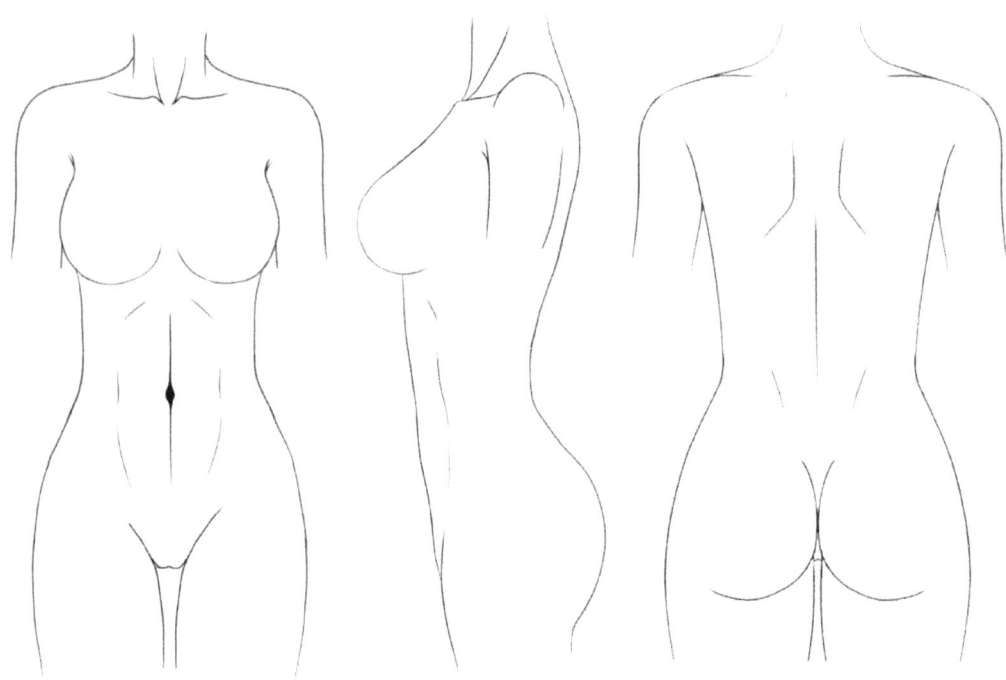

HOW TO DRAW A FEMALE TORSO (FRONT VIEW)

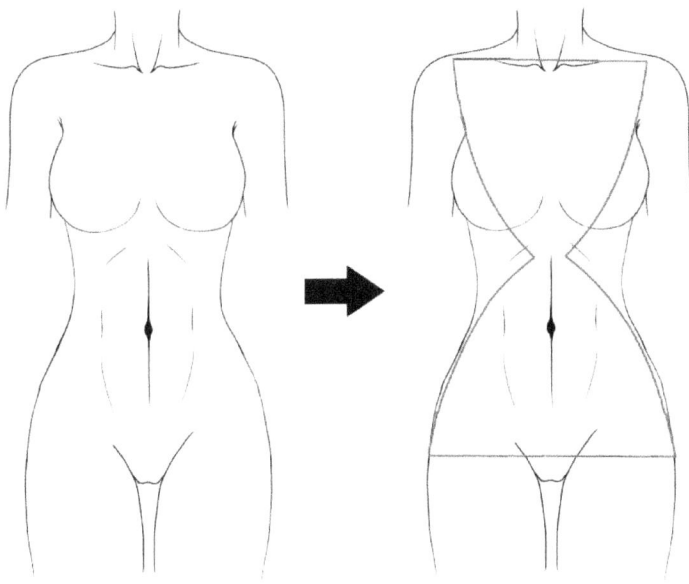

A females torso is like an hour glass shape. The widest part of the female torso is located at their hips. In manga style, the female hips are a little bit wider than normal.

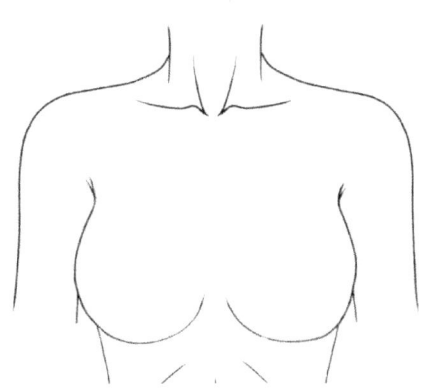

The most noticeable and very crucial part of the female torso in the front view is the breasts. So you must pay attention to how to draw this, drawing them in a wrong way makes your character not pleasing.

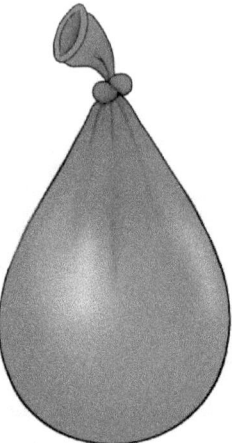

Basically, the structure of the breast is like a balloon half full of water. They have mass and volume so it reacts to gravity

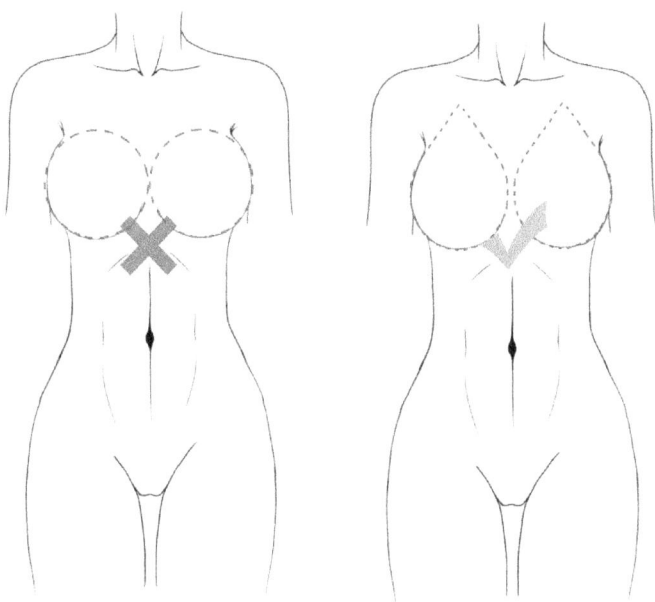

The breast is not round, they are like a teardrop shape. They start to form in the pectoral muscles below the armpit.

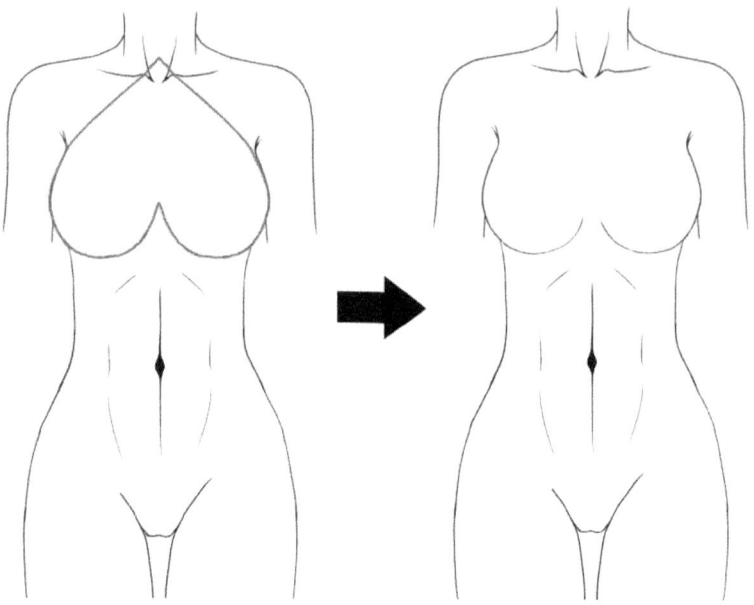

Use an inverted heart shape as a guide , this is an effective technique on how to draw good looking breasts.

HOW TO DRAW A FEMALE TORSO (PROFILE VIEW)

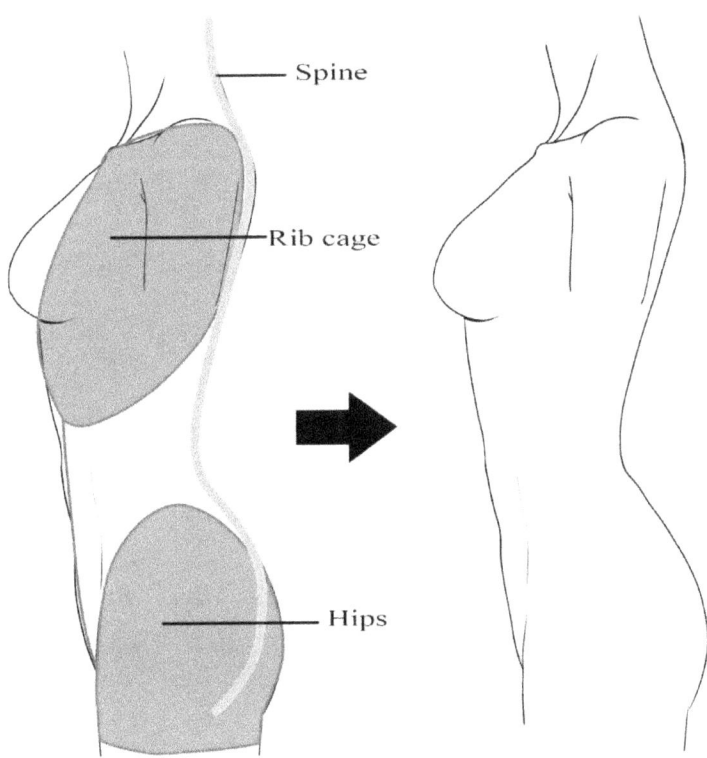

Drawing a female torso can be very tricky at first to a beginner In order to draw a good looking female torso, you must learn the two major things that the torso is made of, the spine and the hard masses (The rib cage and the hips).

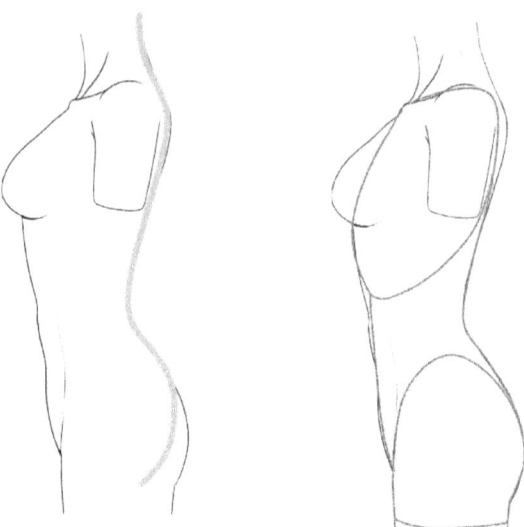

The major mistake that many beginners usually make is in making the spine straight, that makes their drawing look stiff. The spine has random curves, look how it is created in the picture above.

The rib cage is attached to the spine so in relation the rib cage position is dependent to the spine. In profile view, the rib cage is slanted while the hip is in a vertical position.

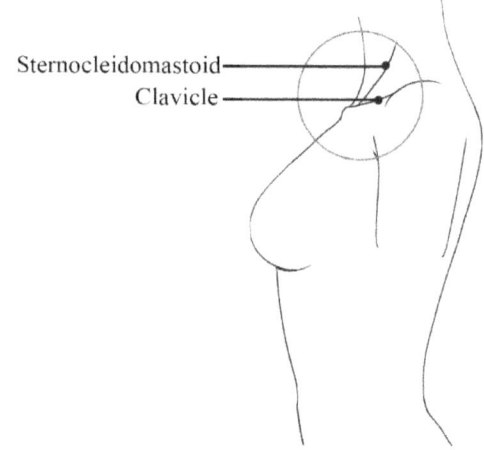

Sternocleidomastoid

Clavicle

Also, pay attention to the neck part don't forget to draw the sternocleidomastoid and the clavicle as shown in the encircled portion.

Drawing a breast in profile view can be simplified by using two lines (a straight line and a curve).

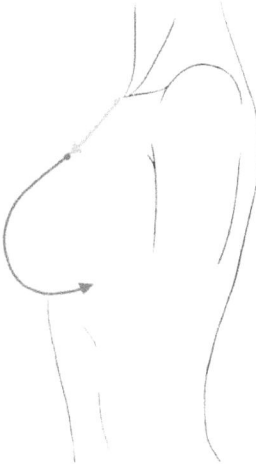

When drawing a big breast, begin with a short slanted straight line at the clavicle, then draw a curve line keep in mind that the big breast has more volume.

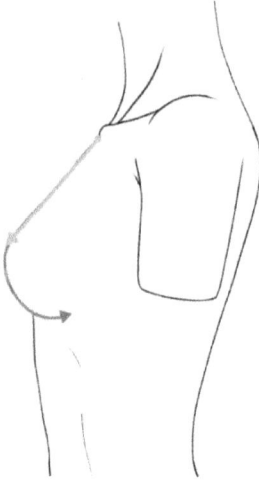

When drawing a small breast draw a long slanted straight line starting at the clavicle, then draw a curve line at the bottom. Small breast tends to look a little bit more pointy.

HOW TO DRAW A FEMALE TORSO (BACK VIEW)

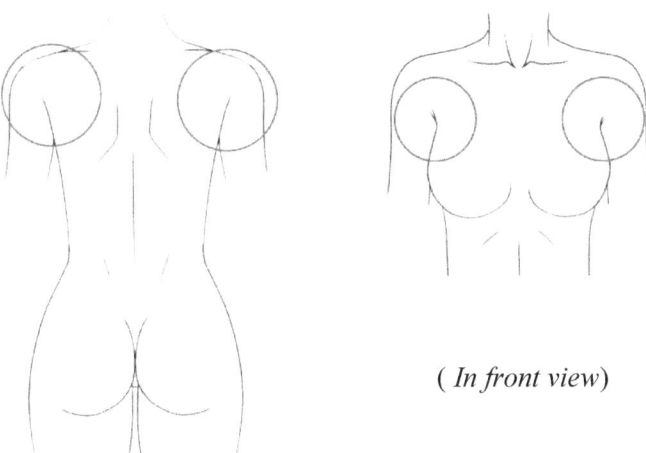

(*In front view*)

The connection of the female torso to the arm is different from the front view, as shown in the picture above.

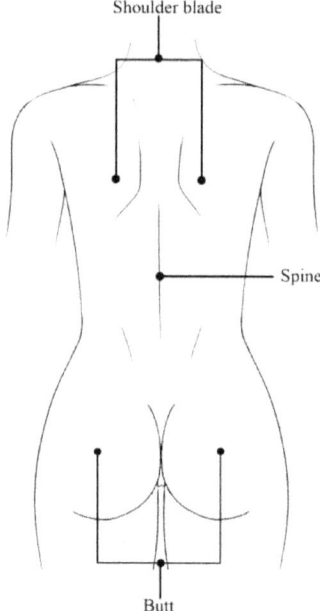

When drawing a female torso in the back view, keep in mind to draw the essential parts as shown in the picture above.

HOW TO DRAW A MALE TORSO IN THREE DIFFERENT VIEWS

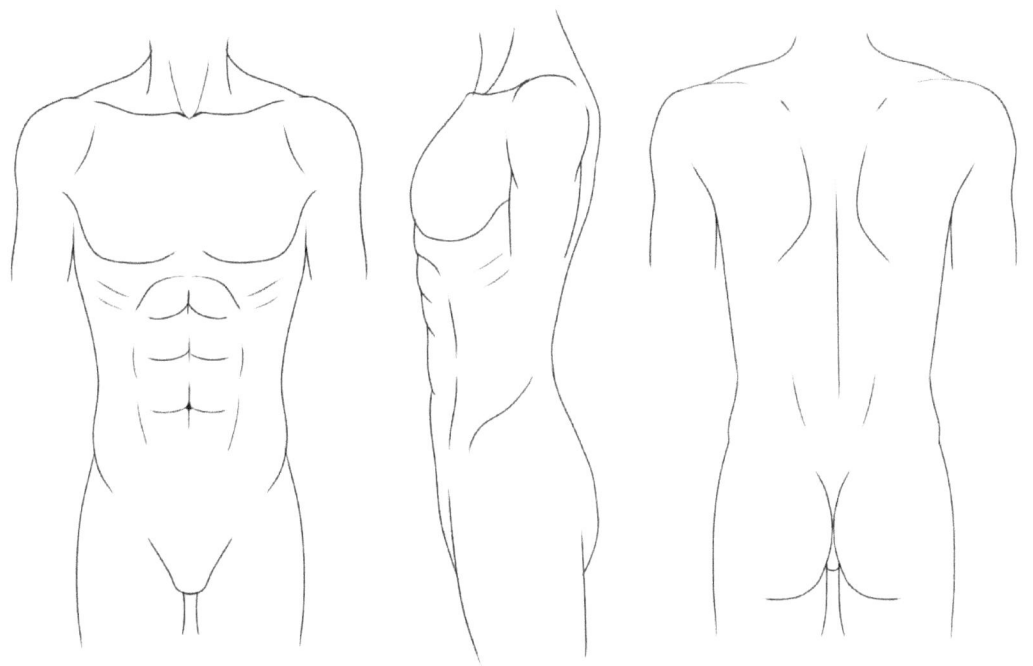

HOW TO DRAW A MALE TORSO (FRONT VIEW)

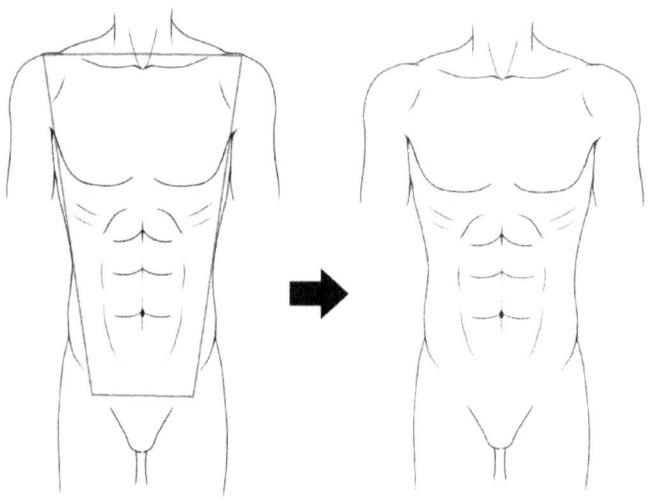

The shape of the male torso can be simplified as an inverted isosceles trapezoid. The widest part of the male torso is located in the chest area.

To differentiate the male torso from the female, defined some of the muscles of the male torso as shown next.

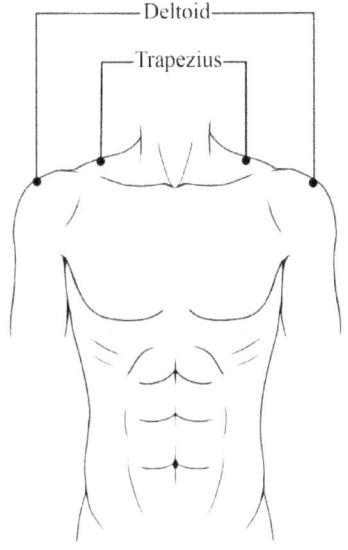

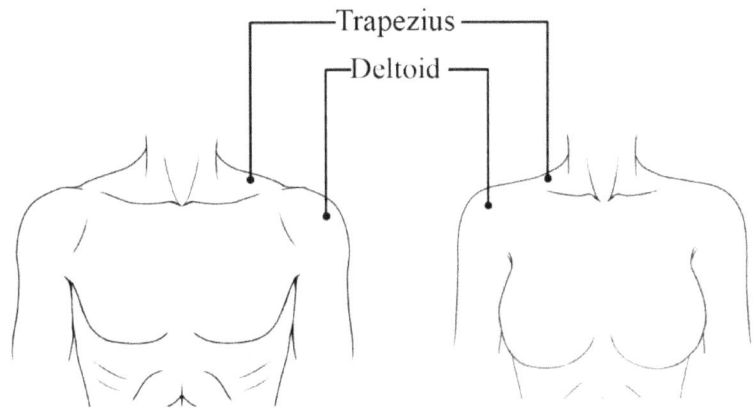

The picture above shows the structure of the Trapezius and deltoid muscles of the opposite gender, by making these muscles more defined and bulkier you'll get a more masculine looking character.

Also, pay attention to the abdominal muscles when drawing a male torso.

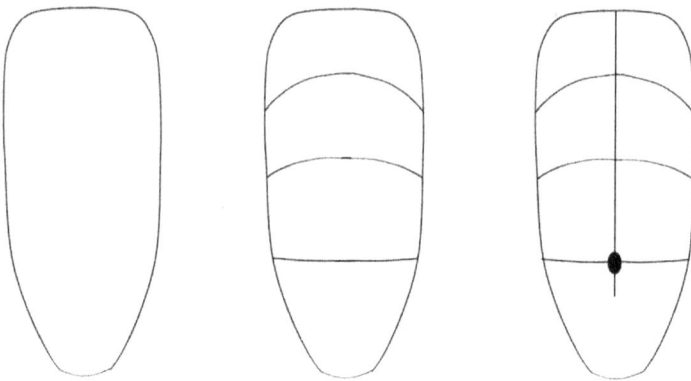

Basically, the shape of the abdominal muscles is like a bottle flipped vertically. It has four layers and the line that creates the division of layers from the top gets less curvy when it reaches the bottom. The line in the middle that divides the layers makes it become a six pack and the lines end below the navel.

To make your character look have more developed abdominal muscles make the shape angular.

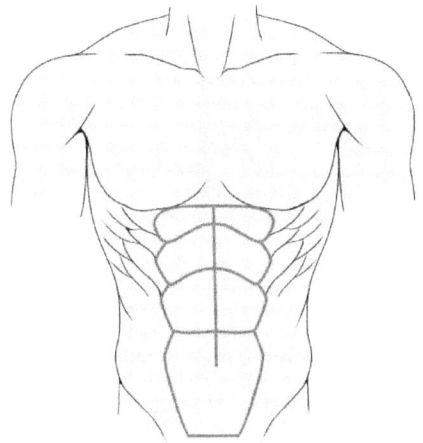

The shadings also, make the abdominal muscles look more defined. Keep in mind to shade the lines darker than the rest, especially in the abdominal muscles.

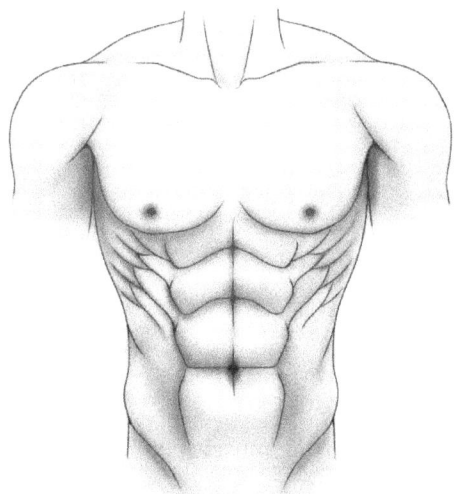

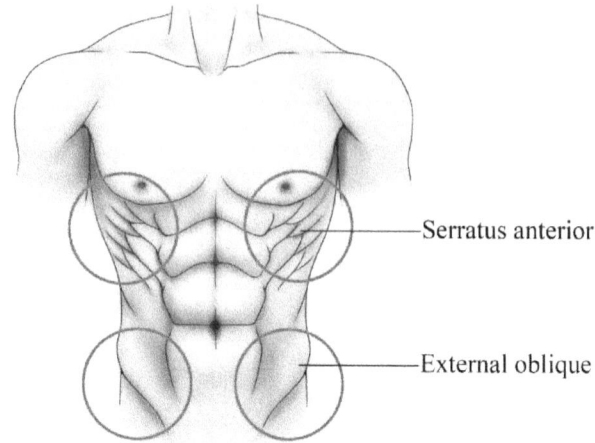

Serratus anterior

External oblique

Also, don't forget to include the muscles beside the abdominal muscles when drawing a character that have well-defined abdominal muscles.

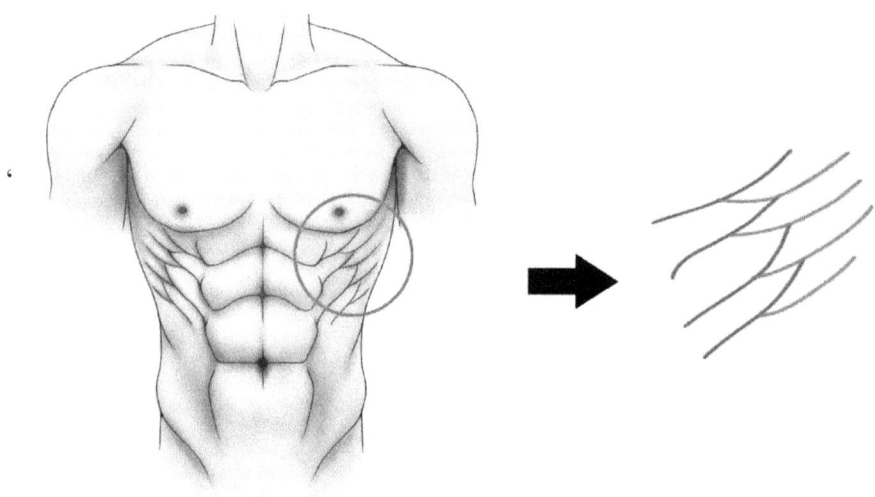

The Serratus anterior weaves the muscles underneath on it and creates a serrated pattern.

HOW TO DRAW A MALE TORSO (PROFILE VIEW)

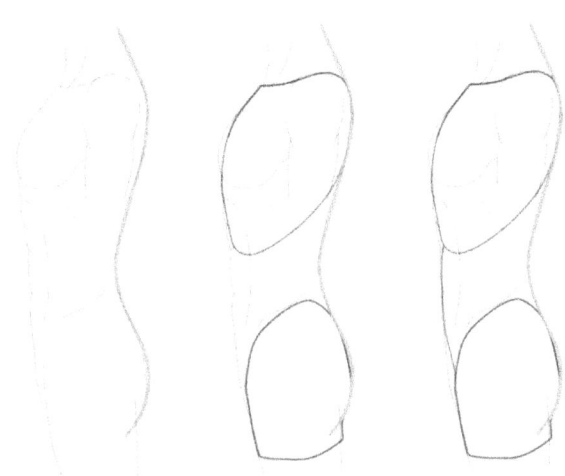

Drawing a male torso is similar to the female as shown earlier.

To differentiate the male torso from female make the spine, less curved, and make the hips smaller and make the butt less defined. Observe the pictuce below to have a better understanding of their structures.

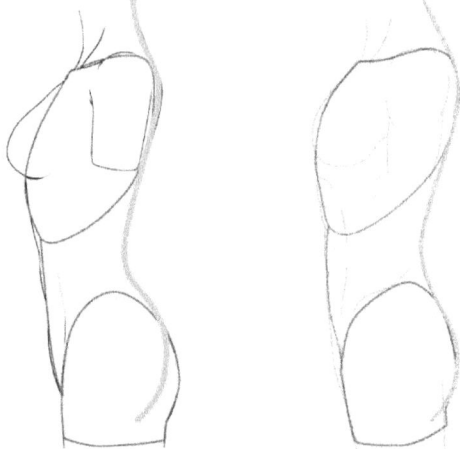

HOW TO DRAW A MALE TORSO (BACK VIEW)

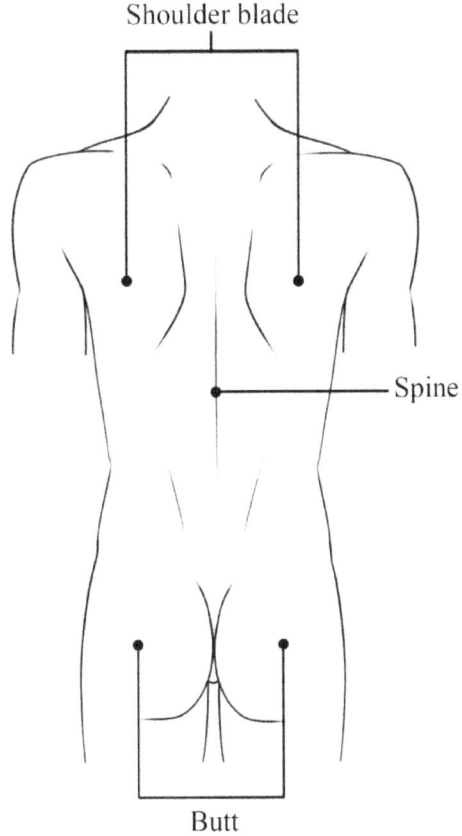

Drawing the male torso in back view is similar to the front view. To differentiate it from the front, draw the essential parts of the torso in the back as shown in the picture.

Keep in mind when drawing the male torso. Make sure the shoulder blades have more definition and make the butt less curvy otherwise, you'll end up with a female looking butt.

HOW TO DRAW AN ARM (ANATOMY AND STRUCTURES)

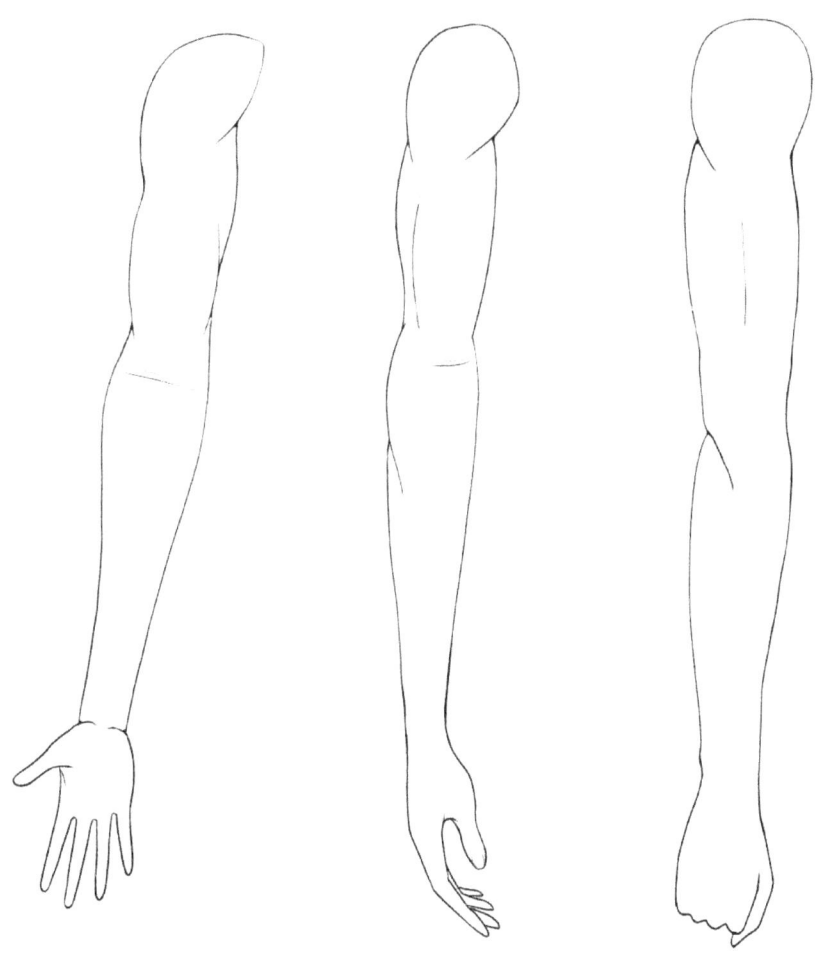

ARM ANATOMY AND STRUCTURE

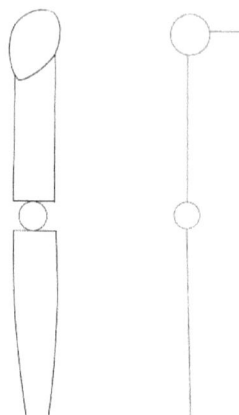

The picture above shows the arm in its basic shape and structures. Drawing an arm can be simplified into stick figures and use a circle to indicate the landmark of the joints.

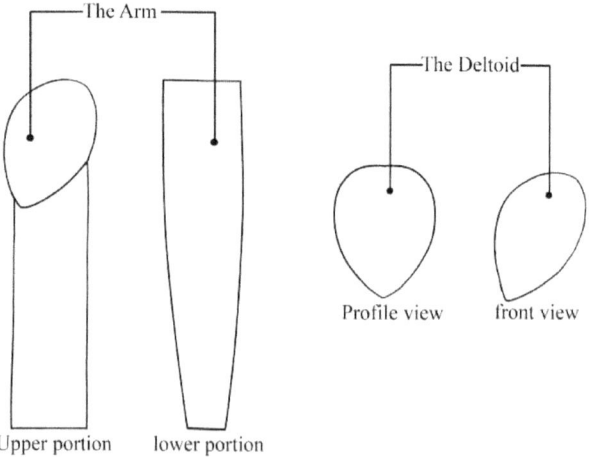

The length of the upper and lower portion of the arm is the same. Keep in mind also that the shape of the deltoid change when the arm is doing a rotation.

When drawing the arm, don't just draw it in its basic structure draw also the muscles around it.

Basically, the upper portion of the arm consists of three major muscles the Deltoid, the bicep, and the triceps.

The muscles of the lower arm can be simplified in three groups of muscles that connect the hand in specific locations

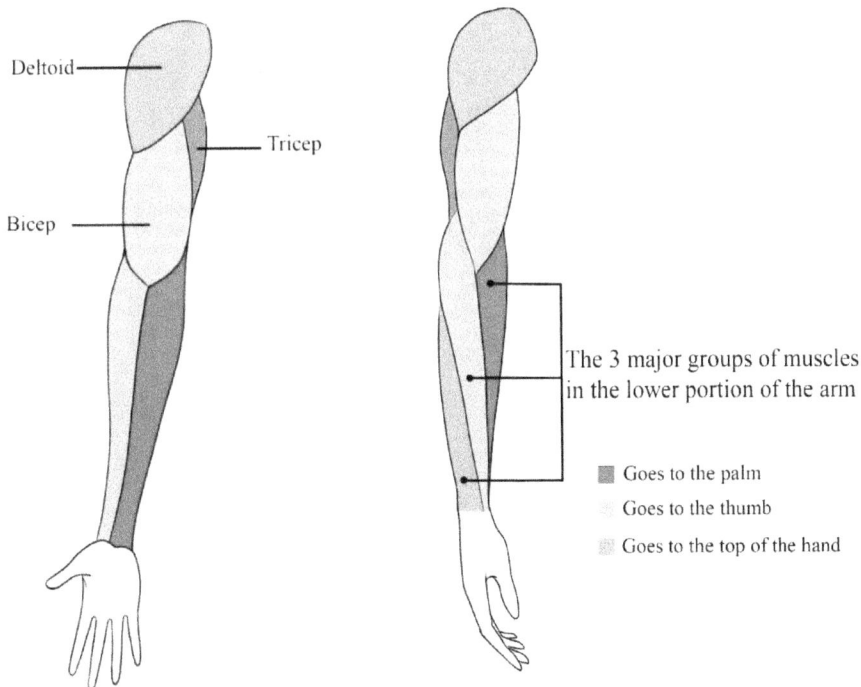

Deltoid

Tricep

Bicep

The 3 major groups of muscles in the lower portion of the arm

▨ Goes to the palm
  Goes to the thumb
▨ Goes to the top of the hand

THE ARM ROTATION

The picture below shows how the muscles move accordingly when the arm rotates. The shape of the muscles in the upper portion of the arm changes as the arm rotates and the muscles in the lower portion of the arm create a twisting motion.

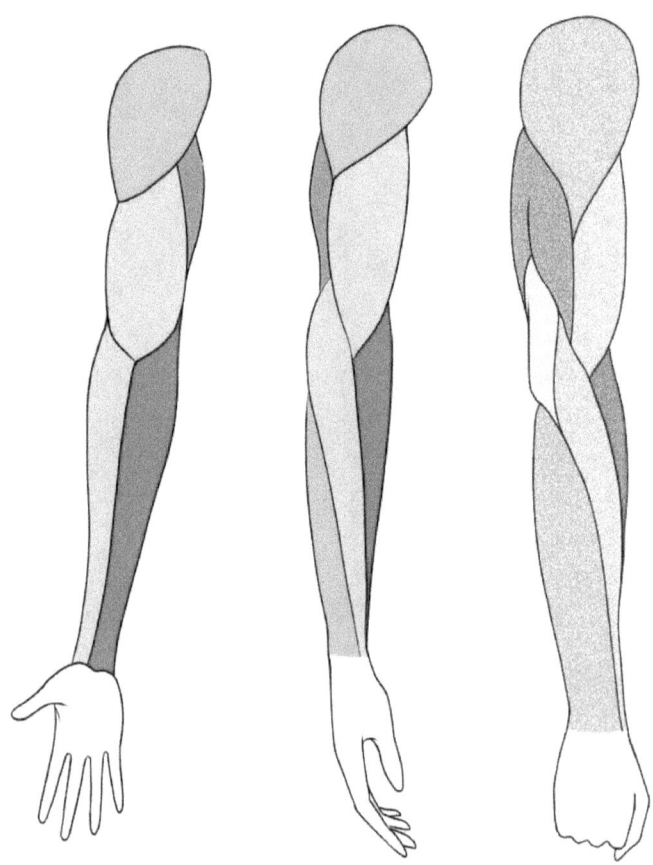

HOW TO DRAW HANDS AND HAND POSES

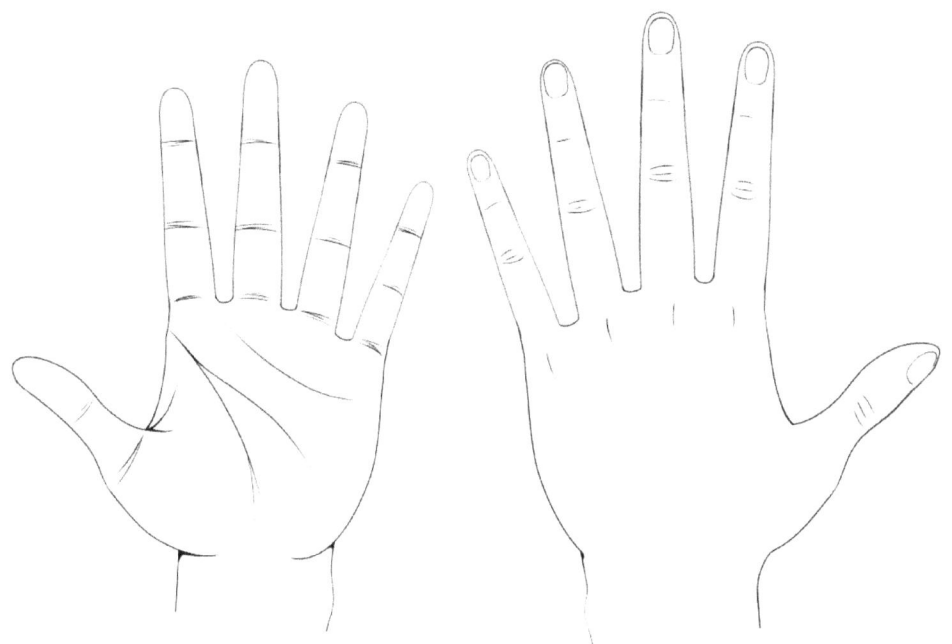

THE HAND PROPORTION AND STRUCTURE

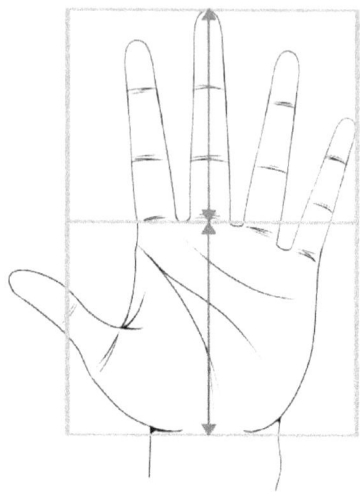

When drawing the hand make the length of the middle finger equal to the length of the palm. Also, keep in mind that the middle finger is the longest finger, the pinky is the shortest, and the first finger and the ring finger can be the same in length or one can be a bit longer.

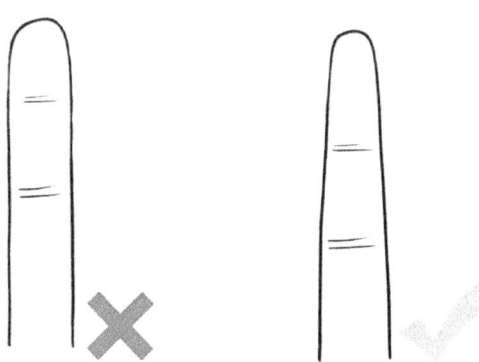

When drawing the fingers keep in mind that the finger is not just a regular cylindrical shape. Fingers are thinner at the top and thicker at the bottom

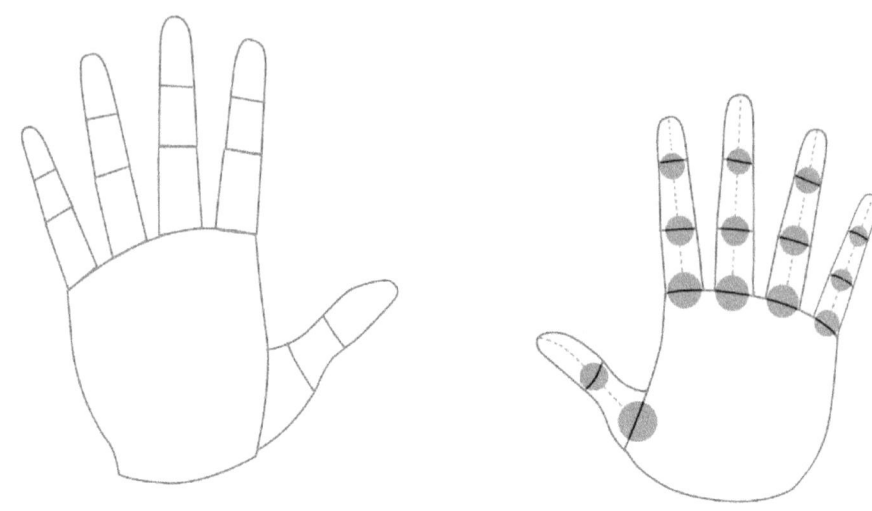

The picture to the left shows the sections of the hand and its basic shapes

Keep in mind that the hand has a joint underneath in it, which make the hands do flexes and the area of the joints makes creases.

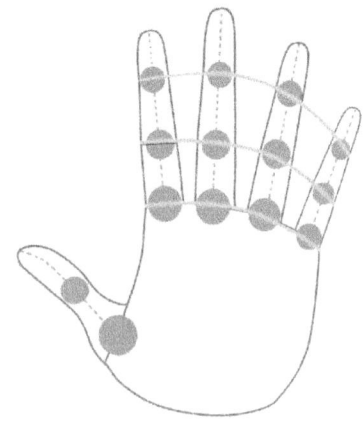

The joints of the hand are not aligned symmetrically they form an arc.

HAND POSES EXAMPLES

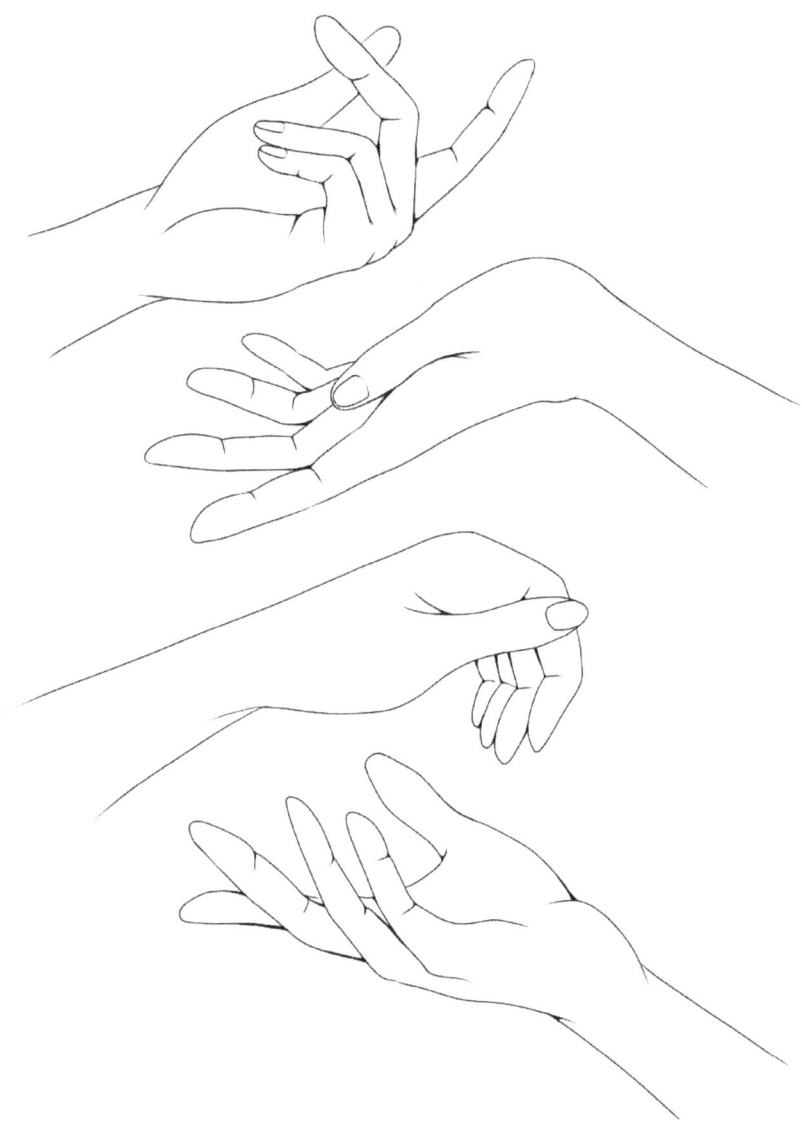

MORE HAND POSES EXAMPLES

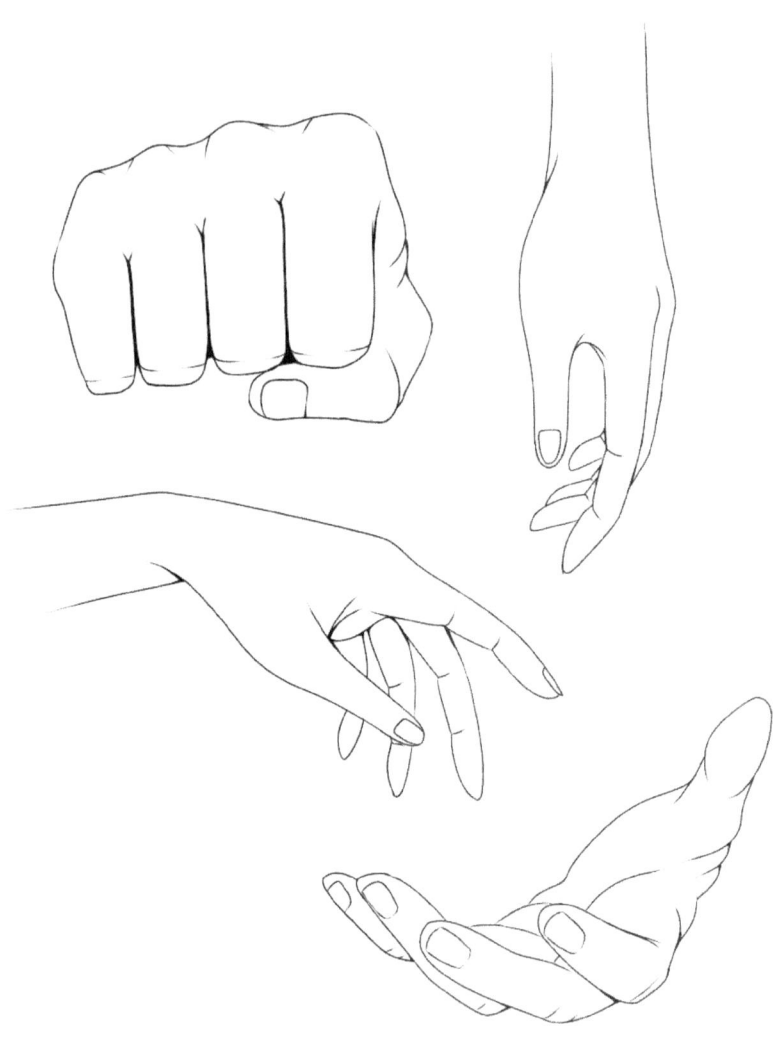

HOW TO DRAW LEGS

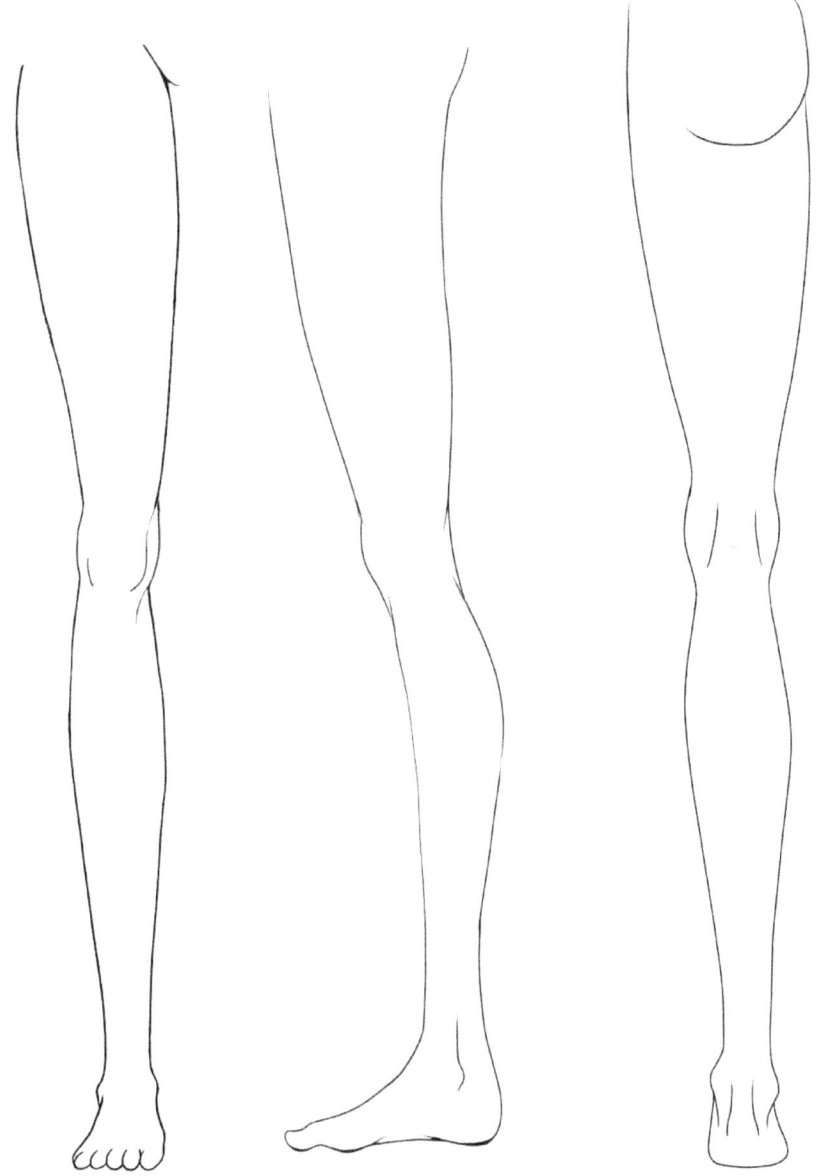

HOW TO DRAW LEGS (FRONT VIEW)

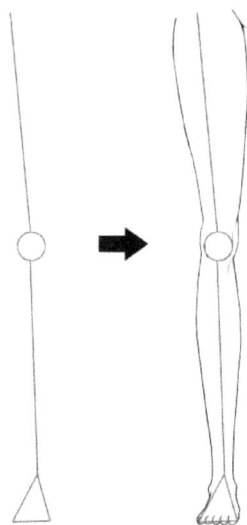

When drawing the legs, first start with a basic stick figure to get the proportion of the legs as shown in the picture above then draw the details.

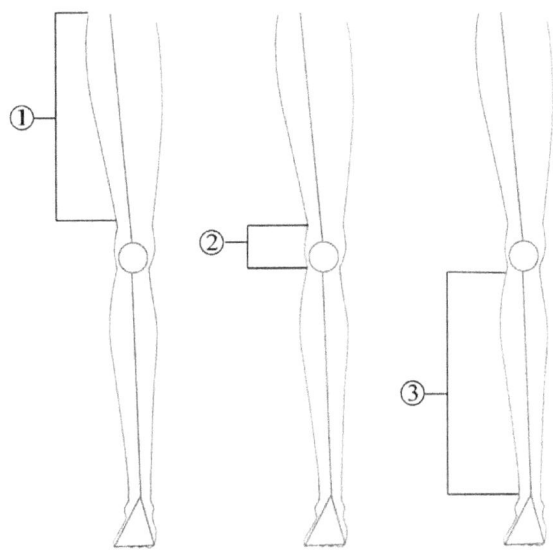

Keep in mind that the sides of the legs are made up of three curves as shown in the picture above

Keep in mind the outer portion of the legs has more defined curves than the inner portion and also don't forget to draw the knee cap when drawing the legs in front view observe how the knee cap was drawn in the picture below

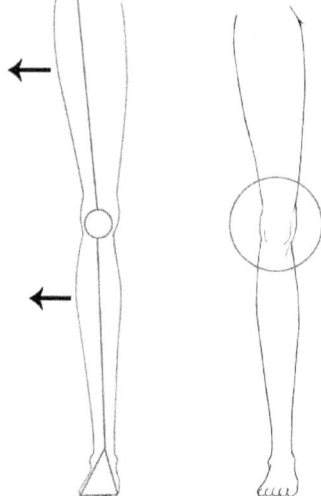

It is important also to learn how to draw legs according to gender. Female Legs tend to look thicker at the top than males. Males have a larger knee cap and more defined calf muscles.

Female   Male

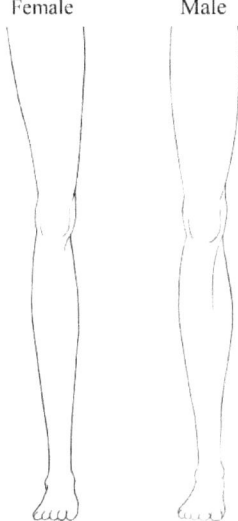

HOW TO DRAW LEGS (PROFILE VIEW)

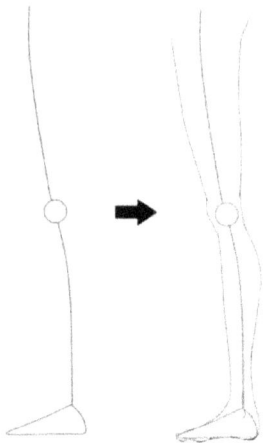

Use an alternating curve when drawing the stick figure as the base when drawing the legs in profile view

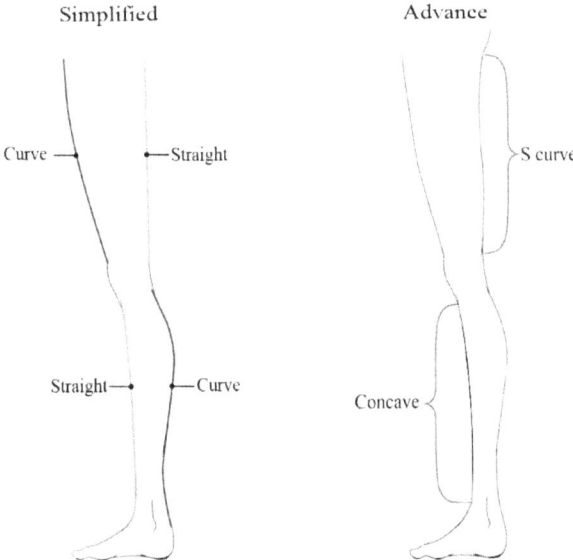

Simplified   Advance

Curve ←   →Straight   ⟩ S curve

Straight→   ←Curve   Concave ⟨

The picture above shows how to construct the lines of the legs in profile view.

HOW TO DRAW LEGS (BACK VIEW)

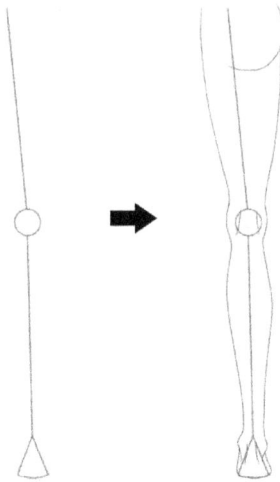

Drawing the legs in the back view is just like drawing as if it's in front view.

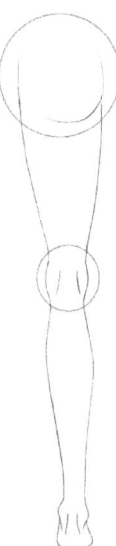

To differentiate the legs from front view, draw the details that make up the legs in back view, the crease in the butt and the tendon at the back of the knee cap.

HOW TO DRAW FEET

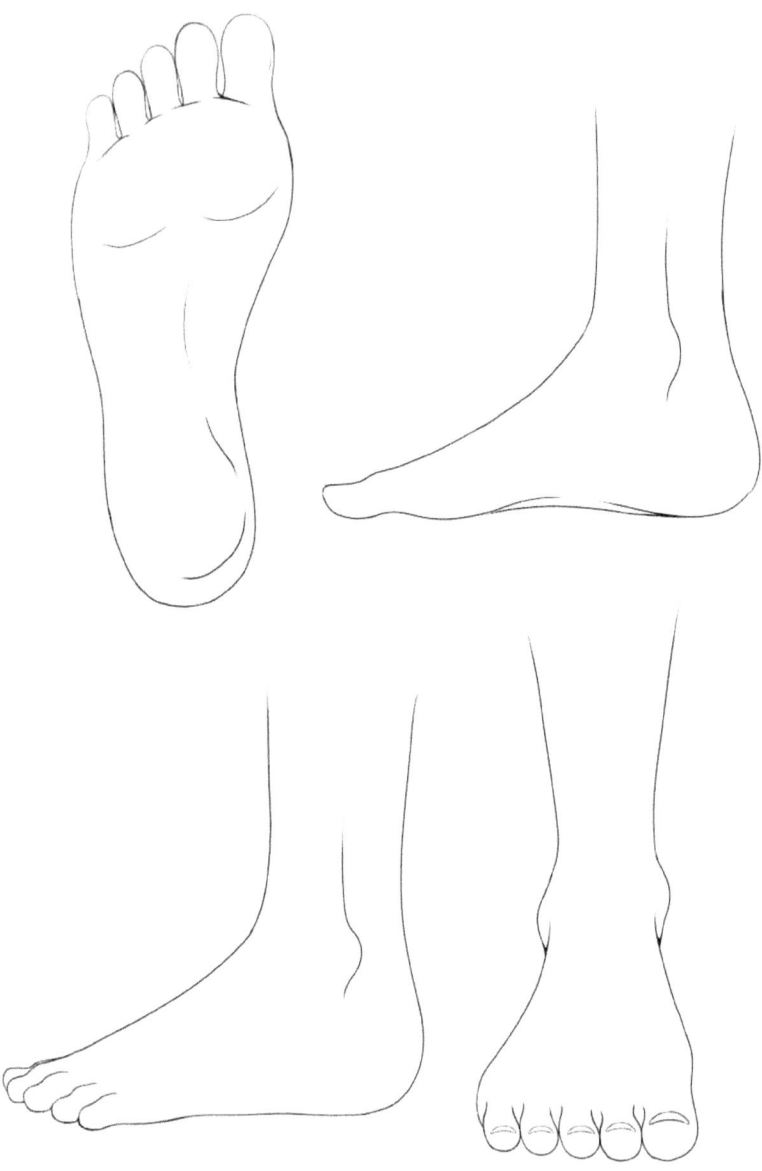

HOW TO DRAW THE BOTTOM OF THE FOOT

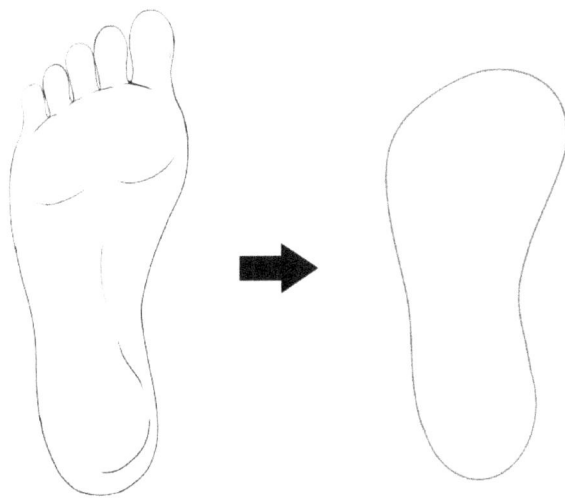

When drawing the feet, know first the structure of the heel. The picture above shows the basic shape of the heel if you get confused drawing the heel at first place follow the method below, first create 2 ovals with different sizes. The bigger oval will be in slanted position while the small oval will be in vertical position, then draw a line that connect to the two ovals

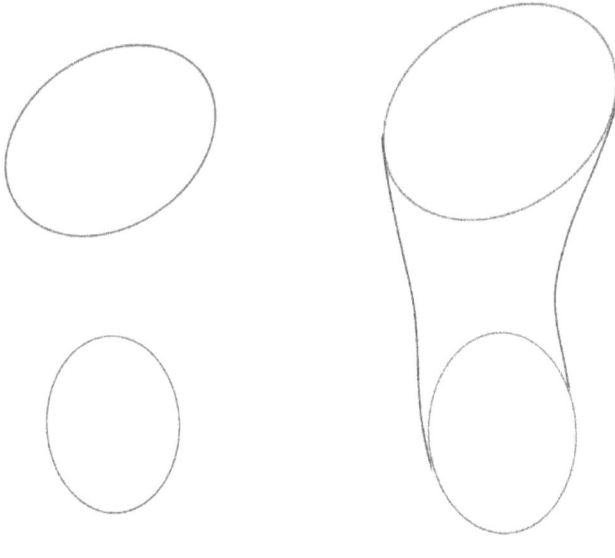

Step 1.   Step 2

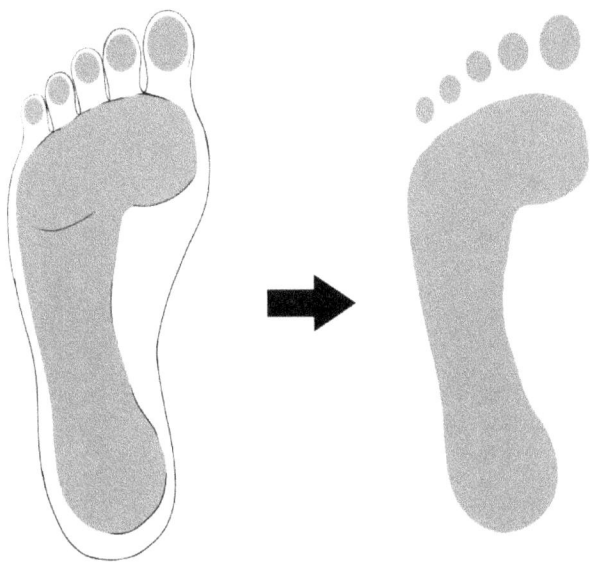

The part that colored in blue is the areas where the foot touches the ground and this area causes the creation of a foot print. It is important to know this area because this will make relation when drawing the foot in standing pose

Below the places that are encircled are the area of the foot that don't touch the ground while the person is standing.

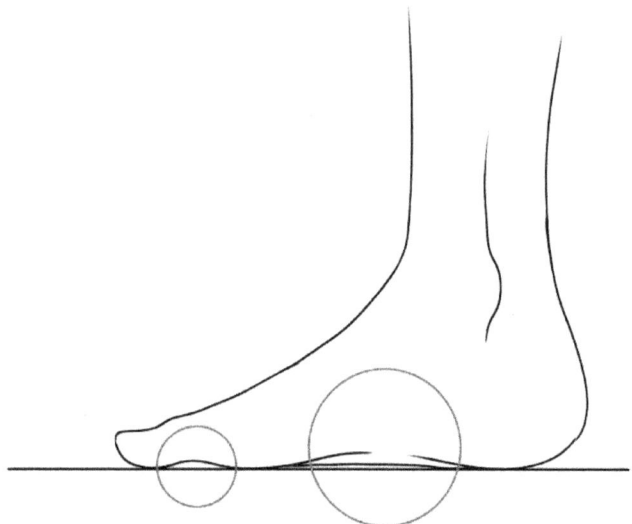

The picture below shows the breakdown of the foot into geometric shape as triangle and circle.

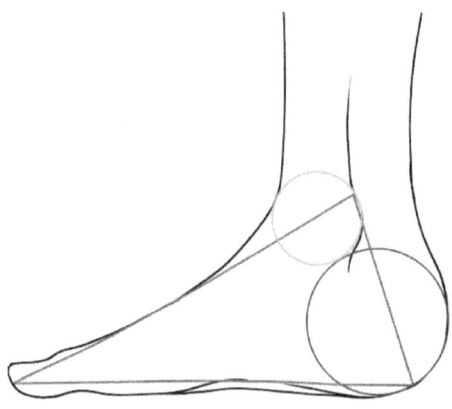

Keep in mind when drawing the top of the toe, make it into three connecting lines not just in one regular line.

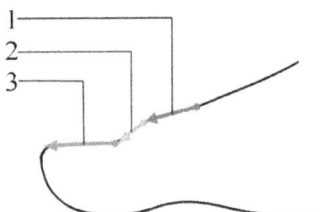

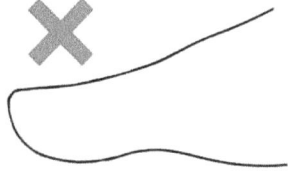

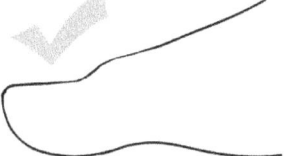

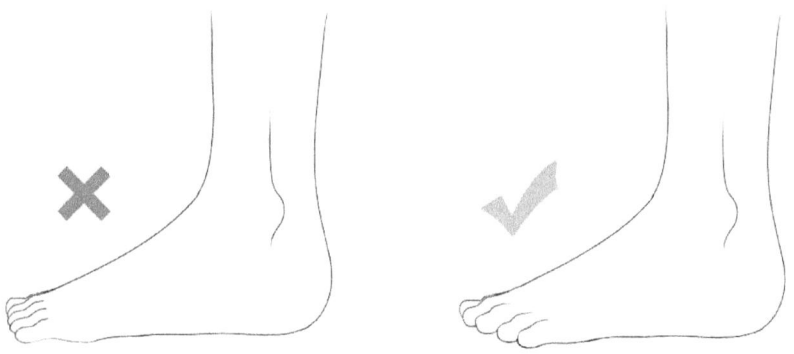

Some of the beginners tend to draw the alignment of the toes in a symmetrical manner. The alignment of the toes is not symmetrical, it falls into an arc and follows the shape of the heel.

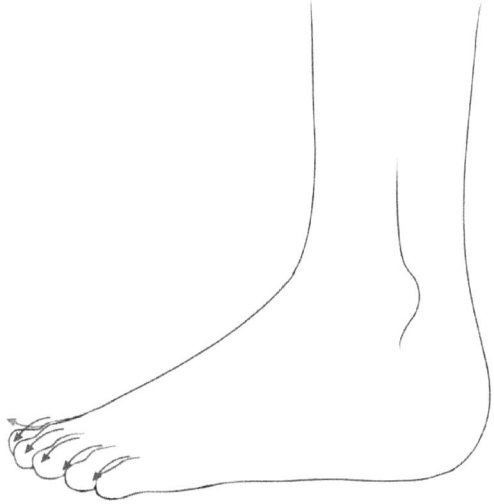

The direction of the big toe differs from the four toes the big toe tends to move upward while the four toes move down and it touches the ground.

DRAWING A FOOT (FRONT VIEW)

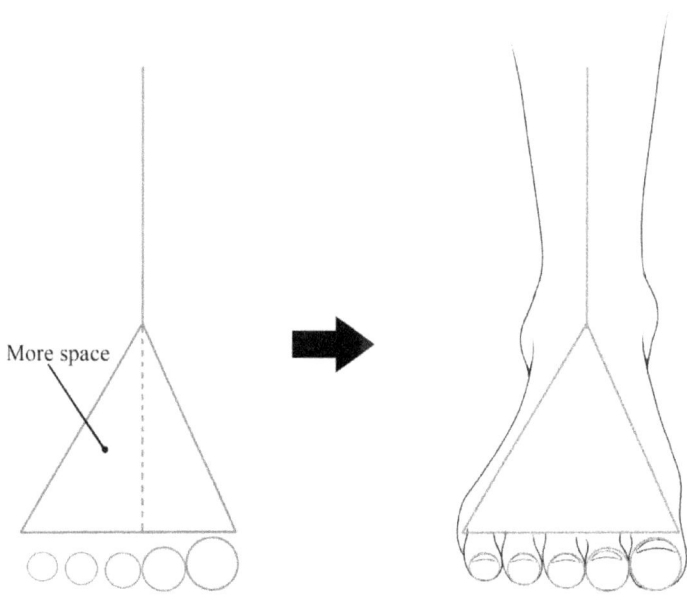

You can use a triangle as a base in drawing the foot in front view, keep in mind that the other side of the triangle is wider that corresponds to the placement of the small toe

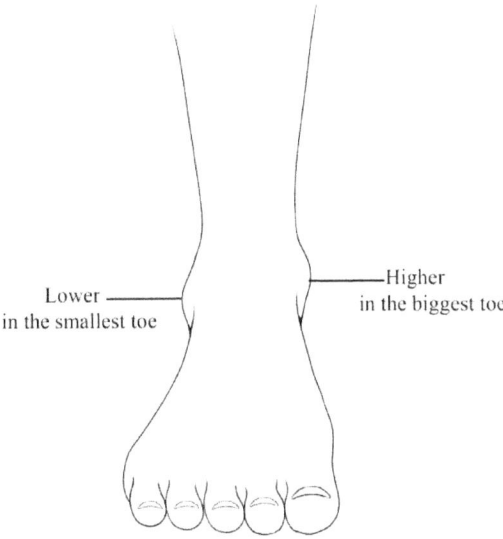

Lower
in the smallest toe

Higher
in the biggest toe

The ankles are not aligned symmetrically they are positioned higher on the other side.

Author Bio

William T. Dela Peña Jr.

William T. Dela Pena Jr. was born in Tondo, Manila but he grew up in their province in Delfin Albano, Isabela. When he was a child his parents and his relatives always get mad at him, because of his unusual behaviour, he is hyperactive and filled with curiosity around his surroundings. He always draws what he see and what he think and from there he discovered his passion for arts. During his school years, he earned a lot of awards in art competitions.

He took BS in Information technology, but unfortunately, he was not able to finish his course due to some reasons. Then he decided to go back to Manila and to work as a graphic artist. While he was working as a graphic artist, he spends his free time in drawing anime then his friends that are Otakus notice that he has a potential in drawing manga then his friend encourages him to get involved in manga industry and he started working as a freelance manga illustrator.

Check out some of the other JD-Biz Publishing books

Gardening Series on Amazon

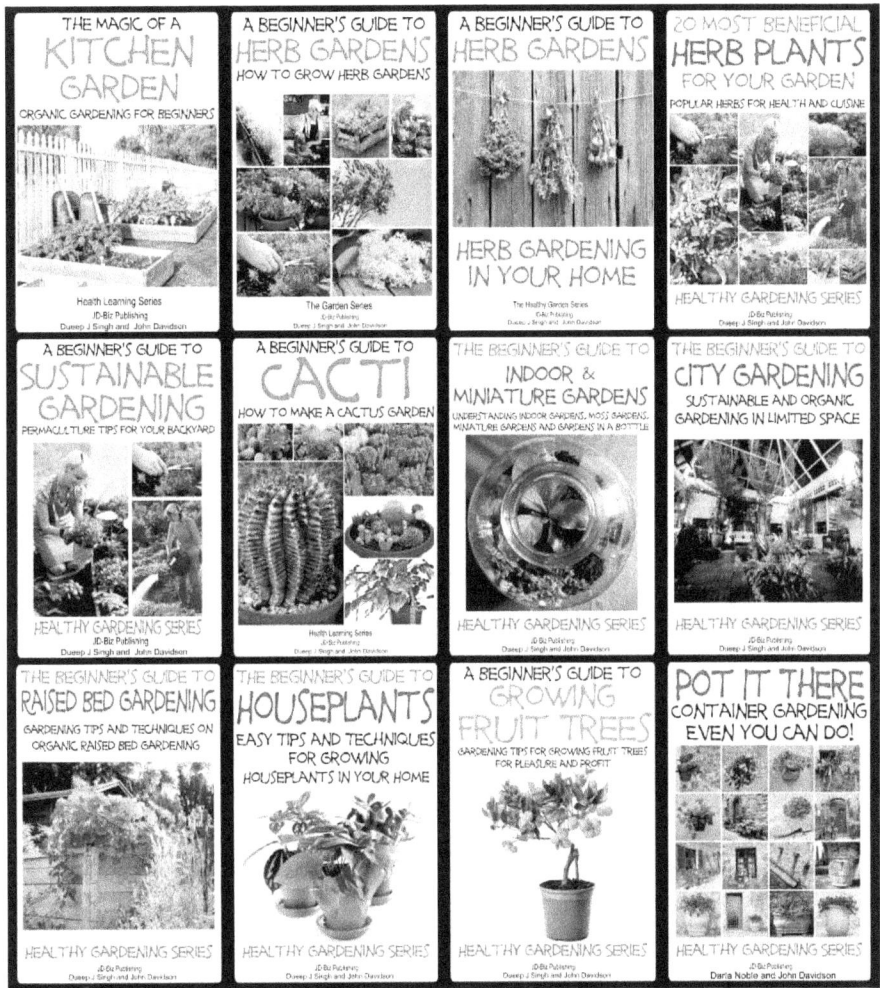

Download Free Books!

http://MendonCottageBooks.com

Health Learning Series

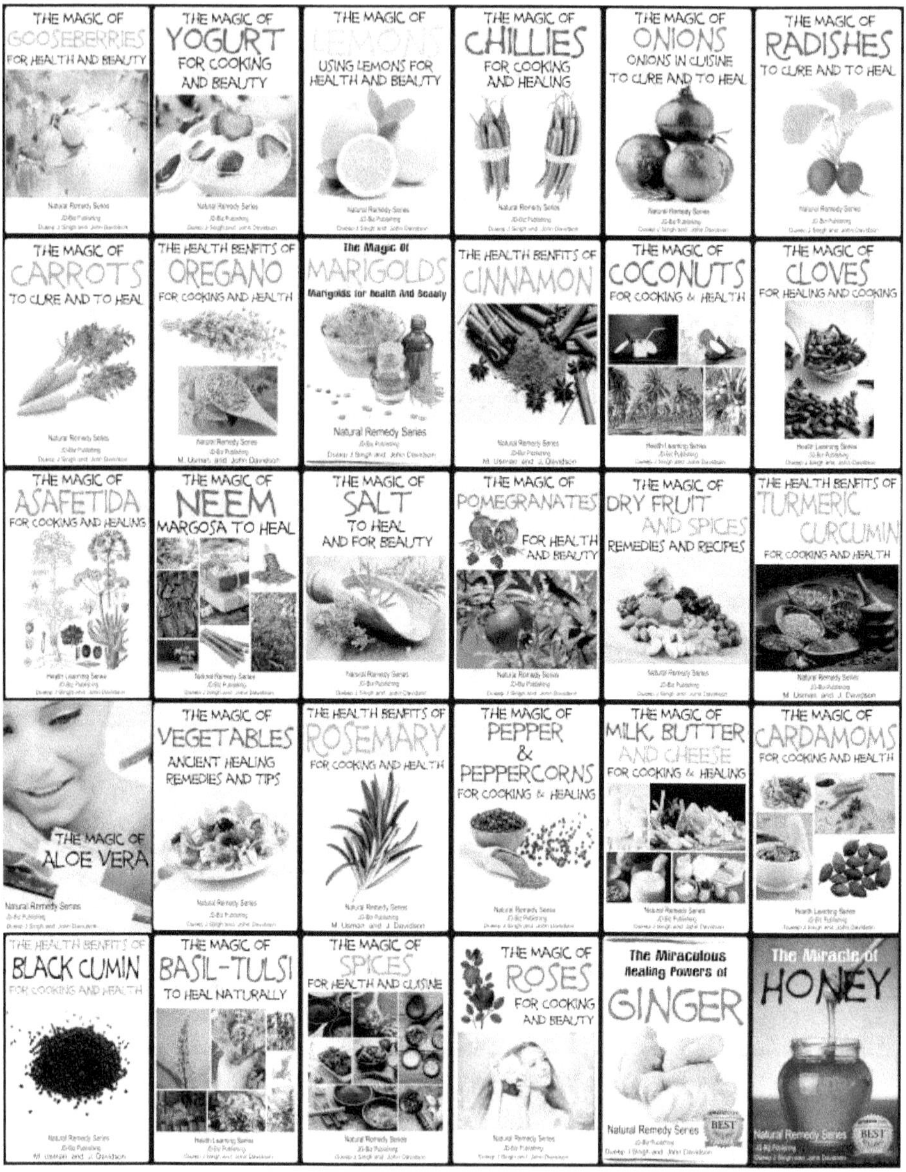

Country Life Books

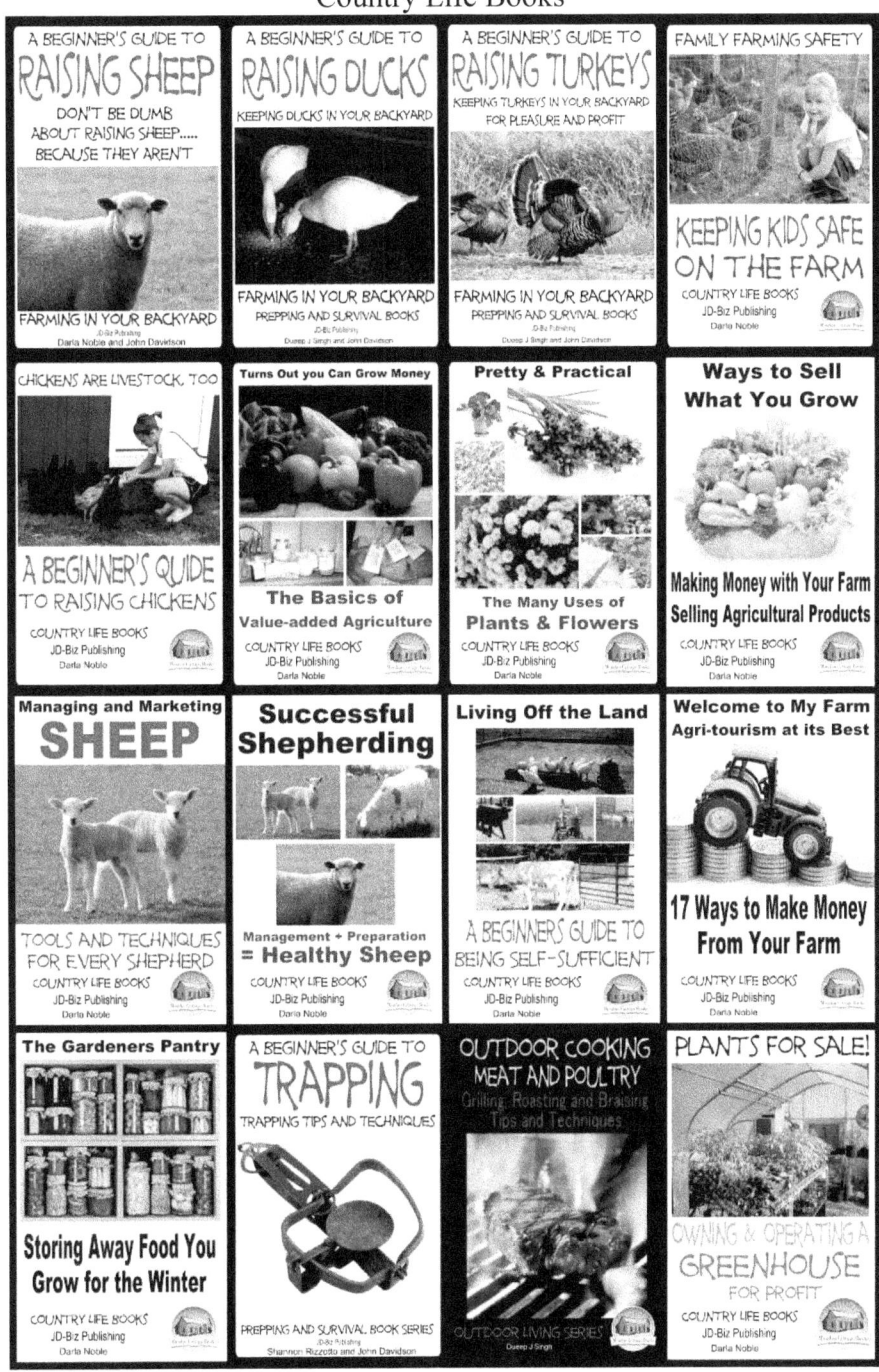

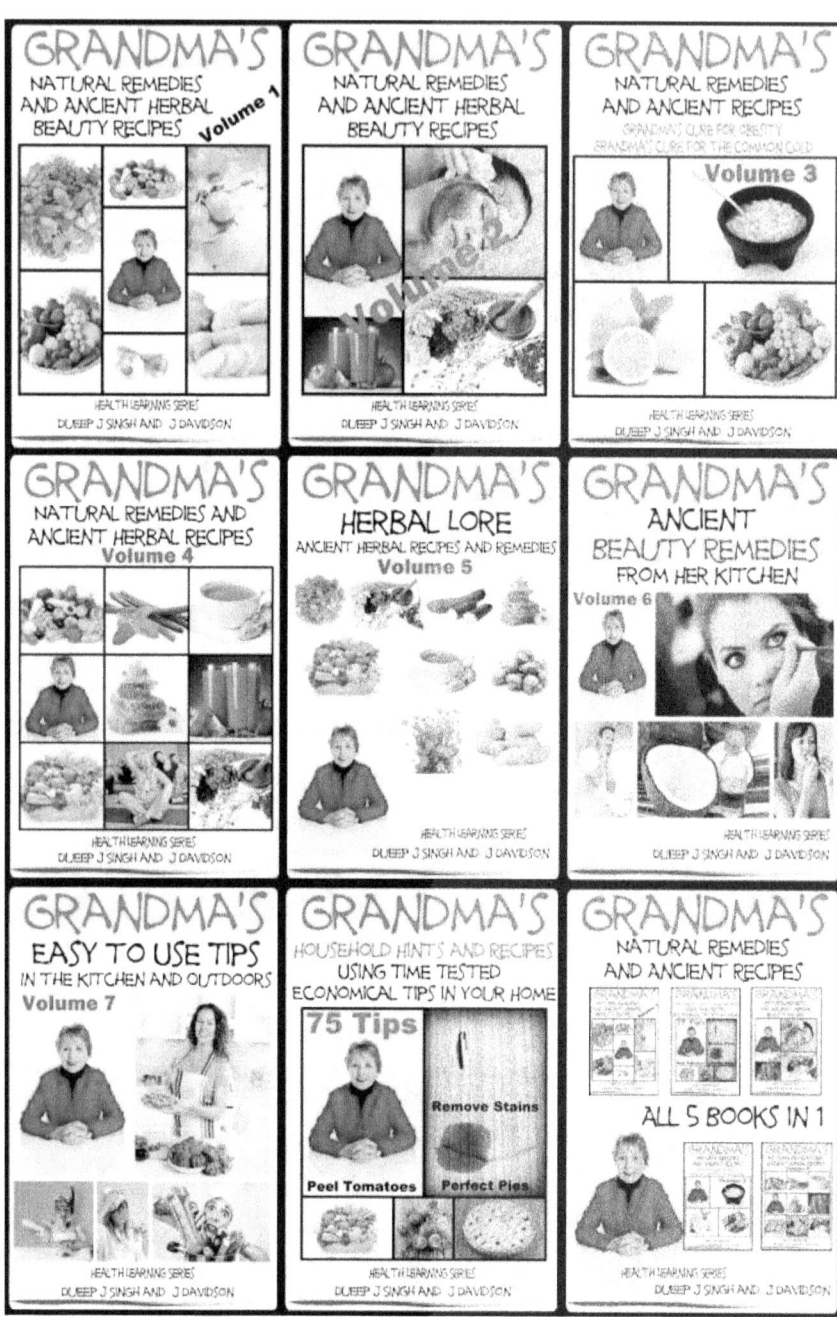

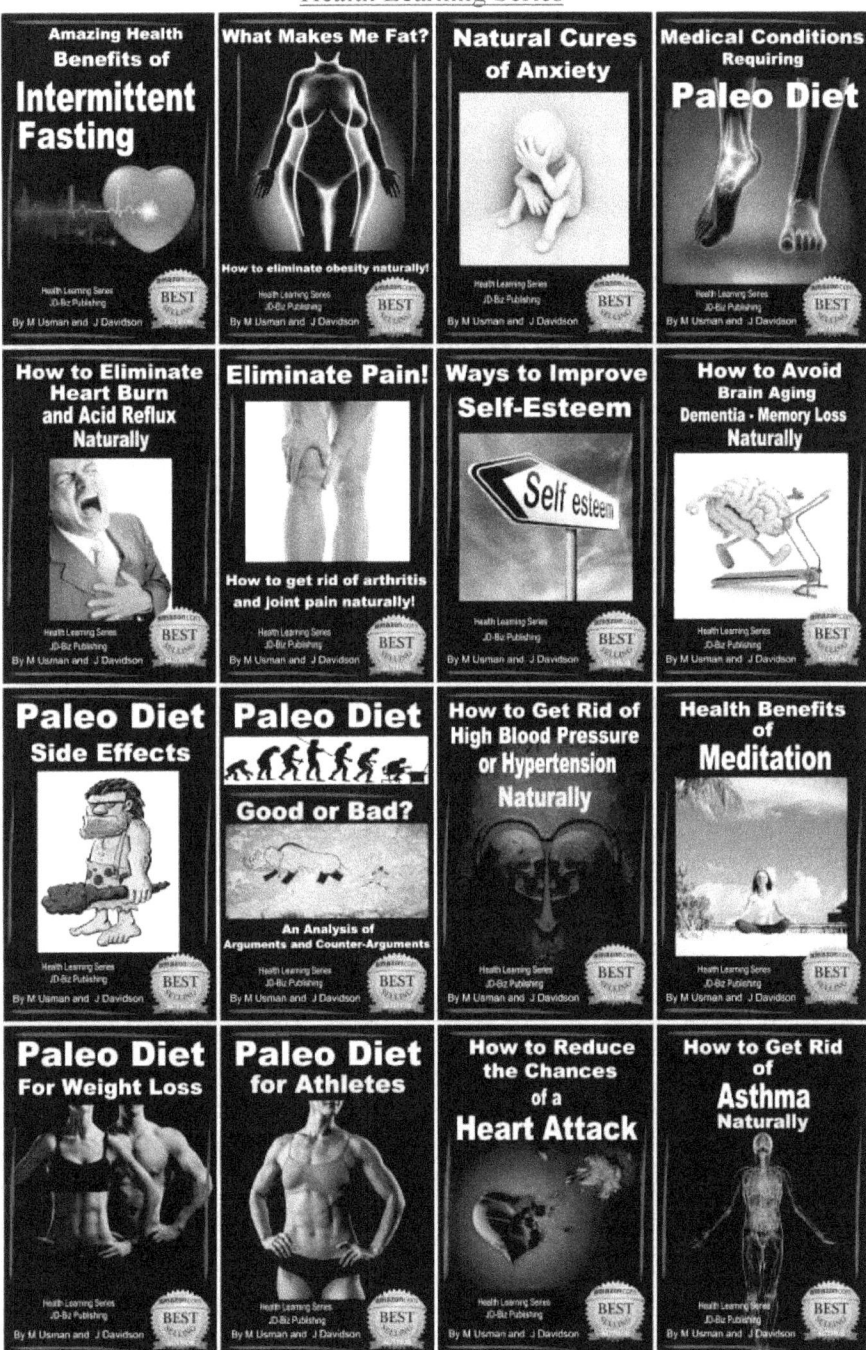

Amazing Animal Book Series

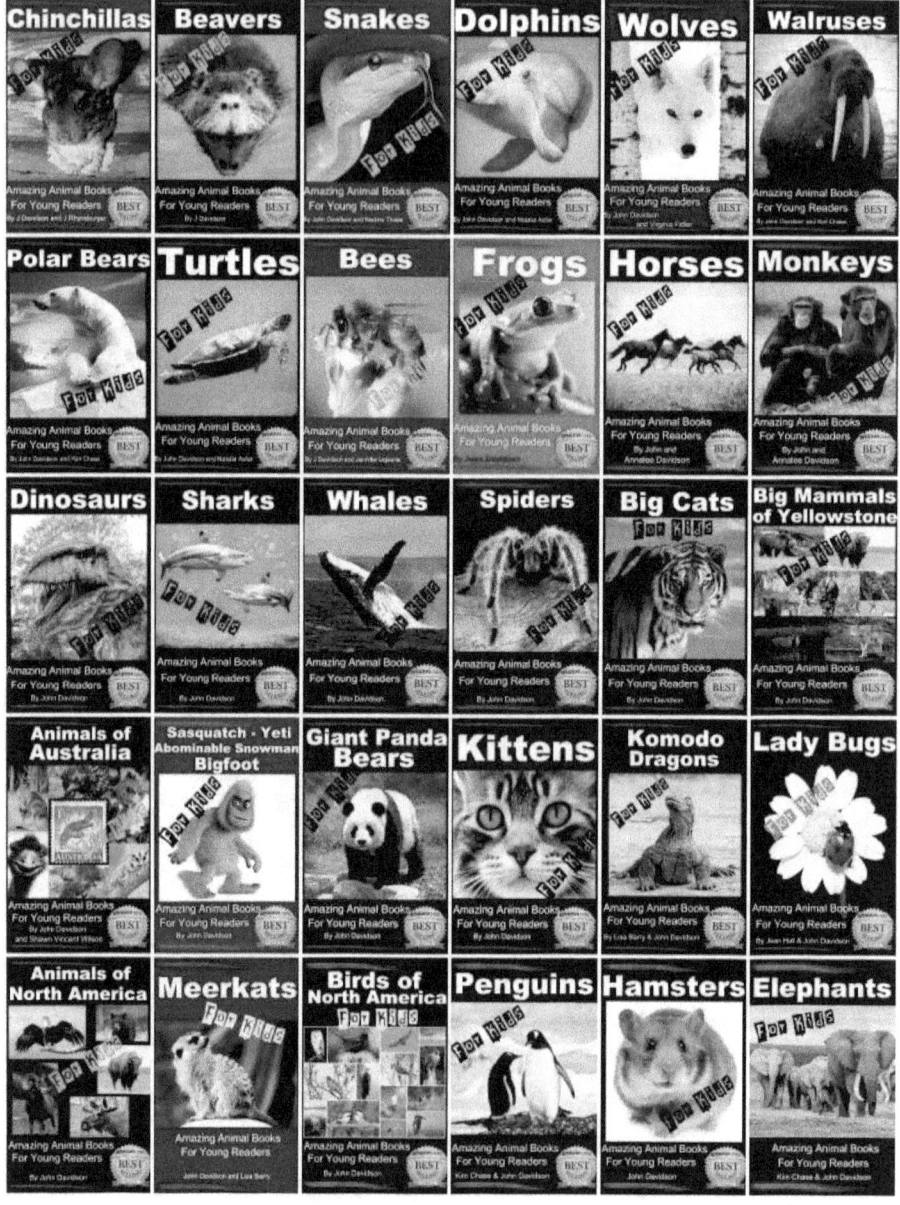

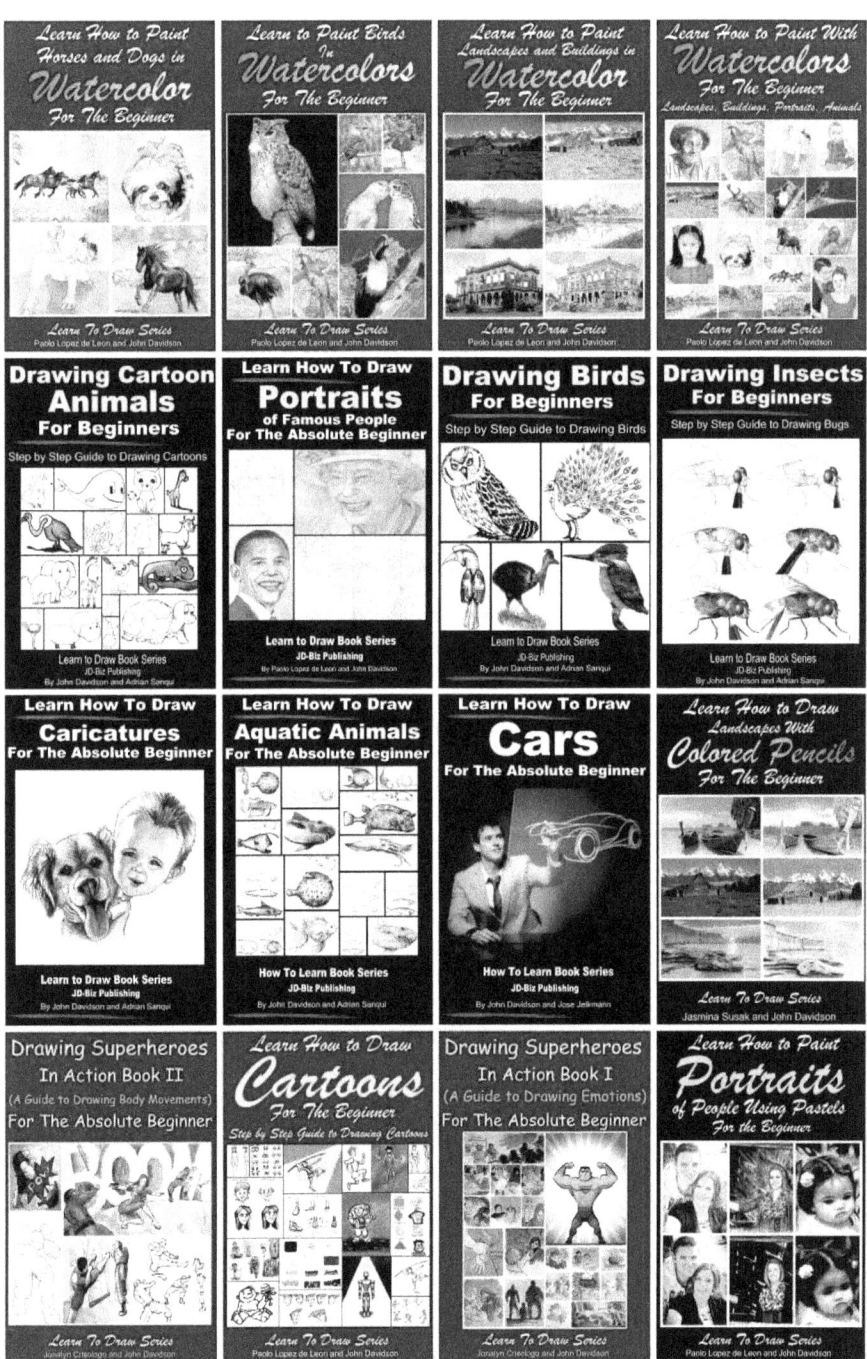

How to Build and Plan Books

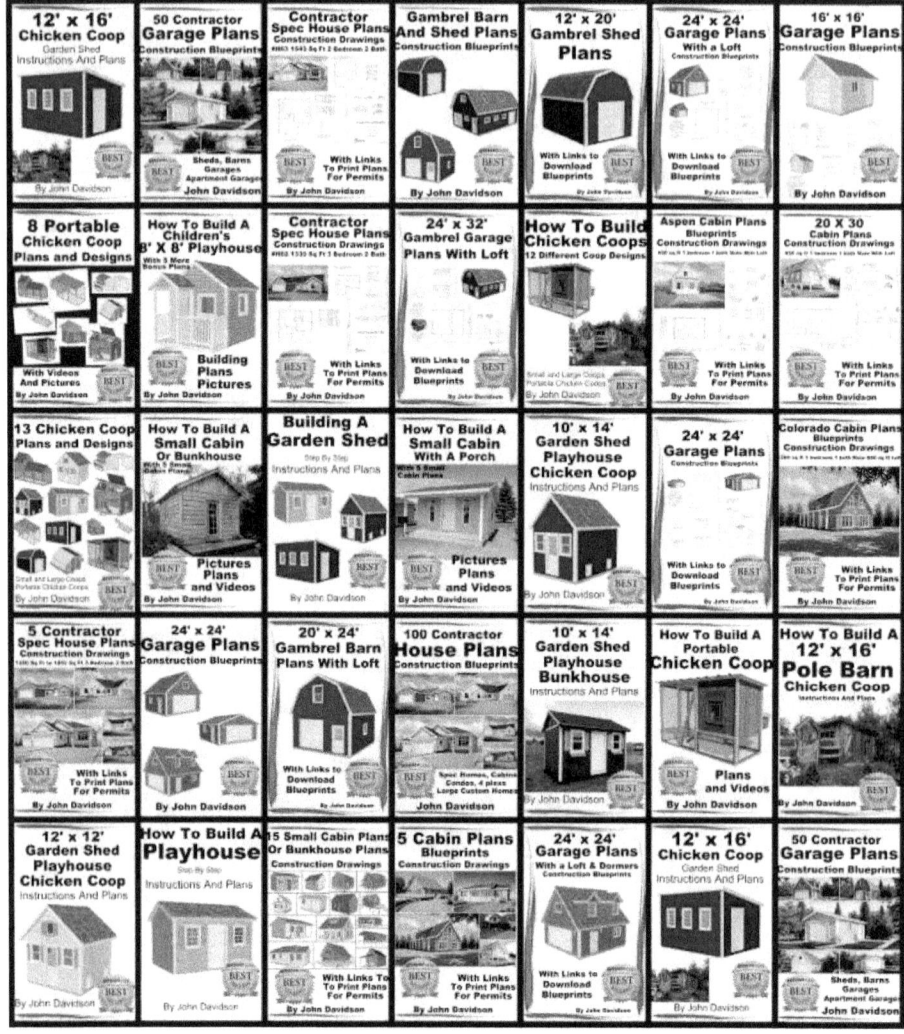

Entrepreneur Book Series

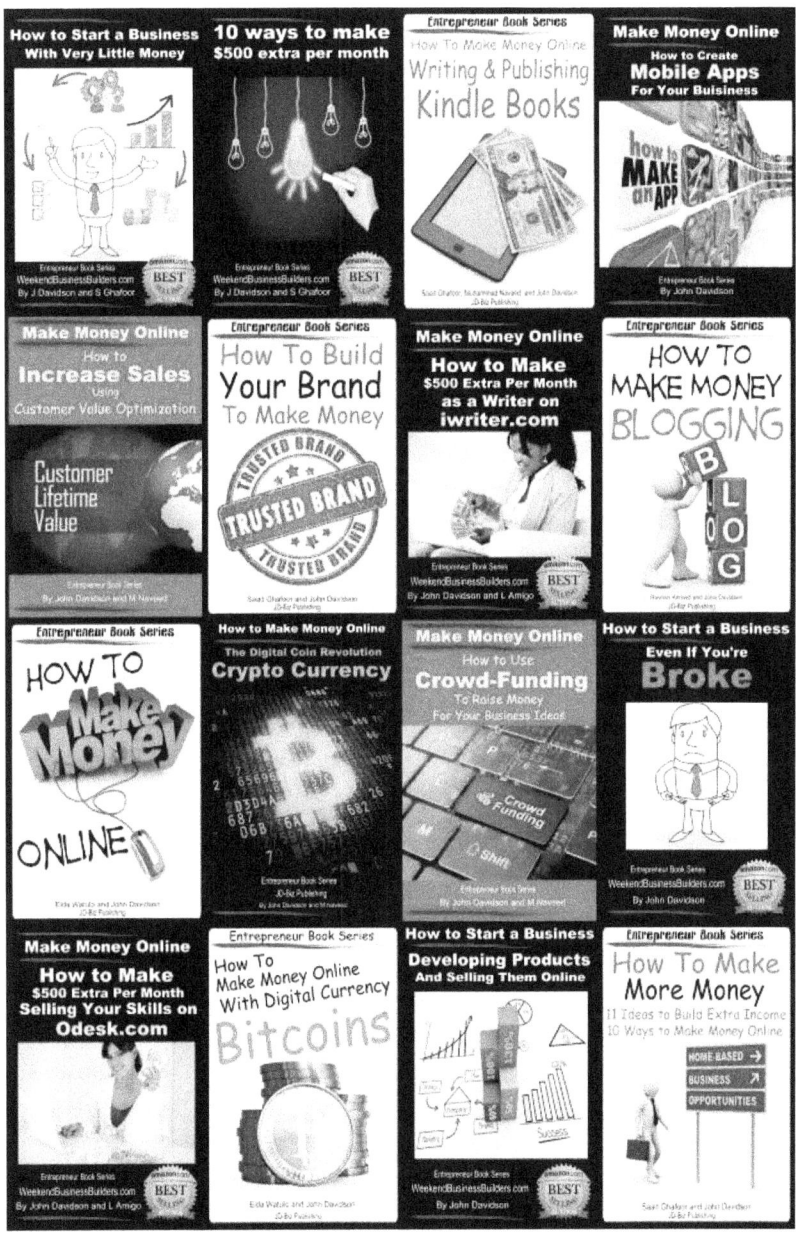

Our books are available at

1. Amazon.com

2. Barnes and Noble

3. Itunes

4. Kobo

5. Smashwords

6. Google Play Books

Download Free Books!

http://MendonCottageBooks.com

Publisher

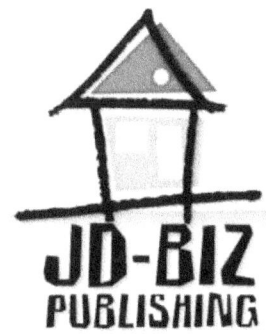

JD-Biz Corp

P O Box 374

Mendon, Utah 84325

http://www.jd-biz.com/

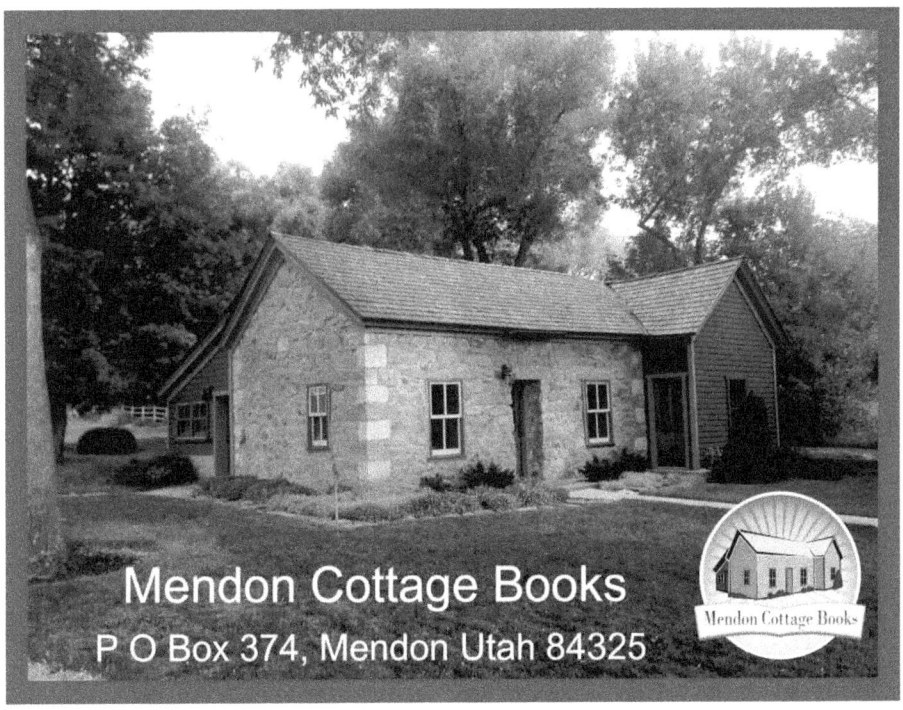